TEXTILES

OF THE

BANJARA

TEXTILES
OF THE
BANJARA

Cloth and Culture
of a Wandering Tribe

CHARLLOTTE KWON and TIM McLAUGHLIN

Over 300 illustrations

Thames & Hudson

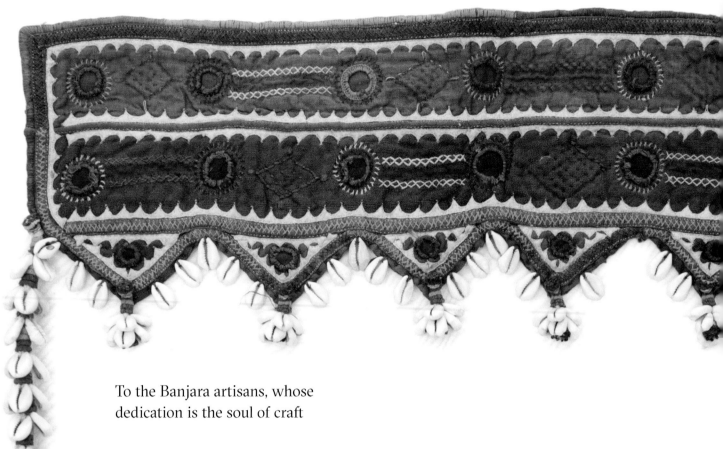

To the Banjara artisans, whose
dedication is the soul of craft

COVER, FRONT AND BACK
Contemporary Banjara embroidery produced by Surya's Garden
(Surya Lambhani-Banjara Women Welfare Trust), 2014. Maiwa collection.

PAGE 1: Woman's *kachali* (backless blouse) from the Shimoga Hills area.
PAGE 2: Detail of woman's *phetiya* (skirt) showing bead and mirror work,
Karnataka.
PAGE 3: Finger rings made from 50 paise coins.

First published in the United Kingdom in 2016
by Thames & Hudson Ltd,
181A High Holborn, London WC1V 7QX

Textiles of the Banjara © 2016 Charllotte Kwon and Tim McLaughlin
Photography © 2016 Charllotte Kwon and Tim McLaughlin

Designed by Tim McLaughlin

British Library Cataloguing-in-Publication Data
A catalogue record for this book is available from
the British Library

ISBN 978-0-500-51837-3

Printed and bound in China by C & C Offset Printing Co. Ltd

To find out about all our publications, please visit
www.thamesandhudson.com. There you can subscribe
to our e-newsletter, browse or download our current
catalogue, and buy any titles that are in print.

CONTENTS

FOREWORD

The Banjara are some of the most visible and yet most mysterious people in India. Distinctively dressed in their astonishing finery, Banjara women are unmistakable figures in the landscape or, nowadays, on building sites, yet few people know much about them. Further confusion arises from the different names by which they are or have been known – are the Banjara synonymous with the Lambanis, for example, or would they be offended to be lumped together? When we admire their textiles, more uncertainty abounds as there are very visually different types of textile that are all labelled 'Banjara' and yet are clearly made by different groups.

Since the 17th century some authors have attempted to define the Banjara and to describe their clothing and jewelry, and certain facts about them are now well known, such as their origins in the caravans that provided Mughal armies with salt, grain and other necessities. Their striking embroideries are included in most books on Indian textiles, but they are almost invariably dealt with in a few sentences (I plead guilty here myself), or, at most, allocated a chapter in a broader book.

The present book is therefore a much-needed deeper treatment of the Banjara and, specifically, their textiles, which draws on years of fieldwork by its dedicated authors Charllotte Kwon and Tim McLaughlin. This book hugely expands our knowledge of Banjara textiles. The boldly coloured, uprooted pieces of mirrored, appliqué and embroidered fabric that so many of us have decorating our homes are put back into their real context and their original uses are defined, illustrated and named. Their distinctive pattern construction, based on squares and border elements, is shown and explained. Unusual and often misidentified items like the tall *chunda* headpiece are not just described but also photographed in use. The authors identify broad regional variations in style and also discuss and illustrate in detail the individual stitches used. For the first time, through both the text and wonderful photographic portraits, we encounter the Banjara as named individuals rather than as an amorphous group, and often recognize them as individuals who have remarkable skills.

It is heartening that these skills are being put to use in the kind of contemporary initiatives described in the book's final chapter. Even if a way of life that includes hanging storage bags and elaborately mirrored garments is waning, the distinctive and beautiful embroideries of the Banjara women are finding a new life. This book not only explains and documents the many textiles of the Banjara, it also shines a light on to their possible future.

ROSEMARY CRILL
Senior Curator, Asian Department, Victoria and Albert Museum, London
June 2015

OPPOSITE
Embroidered square. This piece features many elements that define Banjara embroidery. These include a colour palette with dominant yellows, oranges and reds, geometric designs based on the square with playful asymmetries, filled bands of colour, stitches that cover the ground fabric and an absence of figurative motifs. Maiwa collection, *c.* 1930.

OVERLEAF
Cotton fields near Sigatiranakairi tanda, Karnataka, India, 2013.

PAGES 10–11
Jalavva Lamani, Sigatiranakairi tanda, Karnataka, India, 2013.

the strong thread remains unbroken

1 A STRONG THREAD
The Banjara and their Embroidery

'That is our country', he said, pointing to a tent which covered his grain bags, 'and wherever it is pitched is our home, my ancestors never told me of any other.'

MARK WILKS, *HISTORICAL SKETCHES OF THE SOUTH OF INDIA*, 1817

India is a country known for its cultural diversity and the dramatic appearance of its many ethnic groups. Yet even here, one group stands apart for the beauty of its traditional costume and the forceful presence of its members: the Banjara are a semi-nomadic people who maintain a distinct, self-contained identity.

For several centuries, the Banjara deployed long-distance supply caravans through areas where there were neither roads nor railways. During the Mughal era their lines of loaded animals reached an astonishing size. At the height of their power, droves of 180,000 pack-bullocks were commanded by a single naik (Banjara chief). The caravans transformed the lands they travelled through and could take days to pass a single point. The sizable Banjara camps were known as tandas and this name is still used to identify their modern settlements.

When not employed as the supply train for military adventures, the caravans traded in salt, grains, spices, cotton and rice, acting as independent merchants, buying at the source and selling at the destination. They were a lifeline for trade and essential to India's medieval economy. When the crops failed, famine relief and redistribution of goods depended on their carriage. Farmers courted Banjara visits in order to fertilize their fields and to tap their skills in animal husbandry.

At the close of the eighteenth century the Banjara were engaged to supply the British forces. Lord Cornwallis made use of them during the siege of Seringapatam and the Duke of Wellington employed the Banjara as commissariat staff during his Indian campaigns. The consolidation of British power, however, was to mark the end of the cultural and political conditions under which the nomadic caravans flourished.

OPPOSITE
Arriving from the cotton fields near Sigatiranakairi tanda, Karnataka, Jalavva Lamani wears all her ornament even while performing manual labour, 2013.

ABOVE
A Banjara skirt or *phetiya*.
All over India *phetiya* are
constructed out of the same
basic components, even though
the size of these components
and the fabrics used may vary,
c. 1900, Maiwa collection.

OPPOSITE
Gambibai is a skilled
embroiderer who lives in
Kaddirampura, Karnataka.
She embroiders items for the
Surya's Lambhani-Banjara
Women Welfare Trust (Surya's
Garden) project, 2013.

On the dusty roads of India, the appearance of a Banjara woman is not quickly forgotten. Banjara traditional dress stands out from the daily costume of most other Indian women, which is already a heady and exotic display of festive cloth, of saris, shawls, or salwar kameez made in the most vibrant colours possible. The Banjara, with their voluminous skirts, elaborate adornment, jewelry, tattoos and flowing headscarves, seem to partake of something that marks them as special. Indeed, this is the purpose of most clothing worn by tribal cultures. For those who can read the signs, the patterns of beads, cowries, bangles and embroidery announce a person's community. Such markers also identify a person's position in the community and their family status. In their wealth and type of ornament, the Banjara most resemble the tribal cultures of western India – particularly the pastoral, nomadic Rabari.

But unlike other tribal groups, Banjara can be found in almost every Indian state: from the Punjab in the north to Tamil Nadu in the south, from westernmost Gujarat to the far side of Bengal. In the historical accounts of those who have met them or when identifying themselves, they can go by a bewildering array of names. They participate in all of India's major religions with groups asserting Hindu, Muslim and Sikh beliefs. They follow a variety of occupations from harvesting sugar cane and cotton, to monument building, road construction and agriculture. They are found as members of parliament, lawyers, PhD students and university professors. The Banjara are, in fact, so diverse and widespread that Nora Fisher, the Western anthropologist who spent months among various groups in the late 1980s, felt compelled to ask the important question: 'are these, indeed, one people?'[1]

The vital question of who the Banjara are today is closely tied to how they have been portrayed throughout history, especially during the reign of the British. We have spoken of the Banjara as if they are one group. In fact, a rich diversity of sub-divisions exist, each with distinct religious traditions, lineage, customs and stories. In these sub-divisions there are further separations into major clans. Yet despite this diversity, the Banjara have maintained a remarkable cultural unity over time and throughout the many areas in which they have settled. The Banjara are indeed

RIGHT
Front and back of a small
envelope bag. The life of
embroidered objects such
as this is often complex. The
front reveals that when the
bag was made the seams were
finished with extraordinary
skill, yet the back shows a
crude stitching that deforms
the shape of the bag. It is likely
that some time after the bag
was made a portion of it was
nibbled by a rat or mouse.
The owner stitched the bag
closed in spite of the missing
fabric and created the odd
shape, 18 × 25 cm, *c.* 1900.
Maiwa collection.

OPPOSITE ABOVE
Eleven distinct stitches have
been used in this ceremonial
cloth. Cotton thread, mirrors
and appliqué on indigo and
madder-dyed cotton, Shimoga
Hills, 28 cm square, *c.* 1920.
Maiwa collection.

OPPOSITE BELOW
Square ceremonial cloth.
Cross-stitched cotton thread
on madder-dyed cotton with
border of indigo cloth, Madhya
Pradesh, 35 cm square, *c.* 1920.
Maiwa collection.

one people speaking a common language: Ghorboli.[2] Different groups prefer different appellations (such as Lambadi, Lamani, Laman Banjara, Gor Banjara, Sugali, Vanjara, Wanjara) – some of these names are tied to the cargos that a group specialized in. Lambadi or Laman Banjara are located in the south and were primarily salt carriers. The term Laman is derived from *lavan*, which means salt. The Banjara have an oral culture and so phonetic interpretations have also resulted in a plethora of alternate spellings. We have used Banjara as the most encompassing name.

It is the spectacular nature of Banjara traditional dress, however, that immediately strikes most people. The women, in particular, display a wealth of adornment that appears uncomfortable and inordinately heavy. The arms are more or less completely encased by bangles. A *kachali* (a backless blouse or *choli*) is embroidered with a conspicuous display of mirrors, cowries and pom-poms. The exact placement of items can be specific enough to identify an individual's tanda. A woman's headscarf displays rows of mirrors and coins on the top border. Such scarves are always worn on special occasions. An unadorned scarf might be preferred for daily wear or field work. It is the practice of tying this scarf tightly about the head in such a way as to keep their hair in place that makes the women most resemble their distant cousins – the European Roma.

Banjara embroider in a way that reflects who they are. The designs are bold and immediate. The lines and shapes have strength of personality that permits them to wander over the surface of a work without diminishing their distinctive character. Stitchwork alludes to symmetry without being symmetric and manages to incorporate geometric principles only loosely. Embroideries by tribal groups in India's Kachchh Desert often display an exact, jewel-like quality, but this quality is mostly absent from Banjara work. Banjara embroideries, like the Banjara themselves, are almost instantly identifiable. The fortitude of the patterns and the wealth of stitches is unmatched by any other culture.

OPPOSITE

Kachali, an exceptional example of the dense mirror placement that characterizes embroidery from the Shimoga Hills area, *c.* 1960. John Childs collection.

BELOW

Detail of new work being done by Surya's Garden located in Kaddirampura, Karnataka, 2012. Maiwa collection.

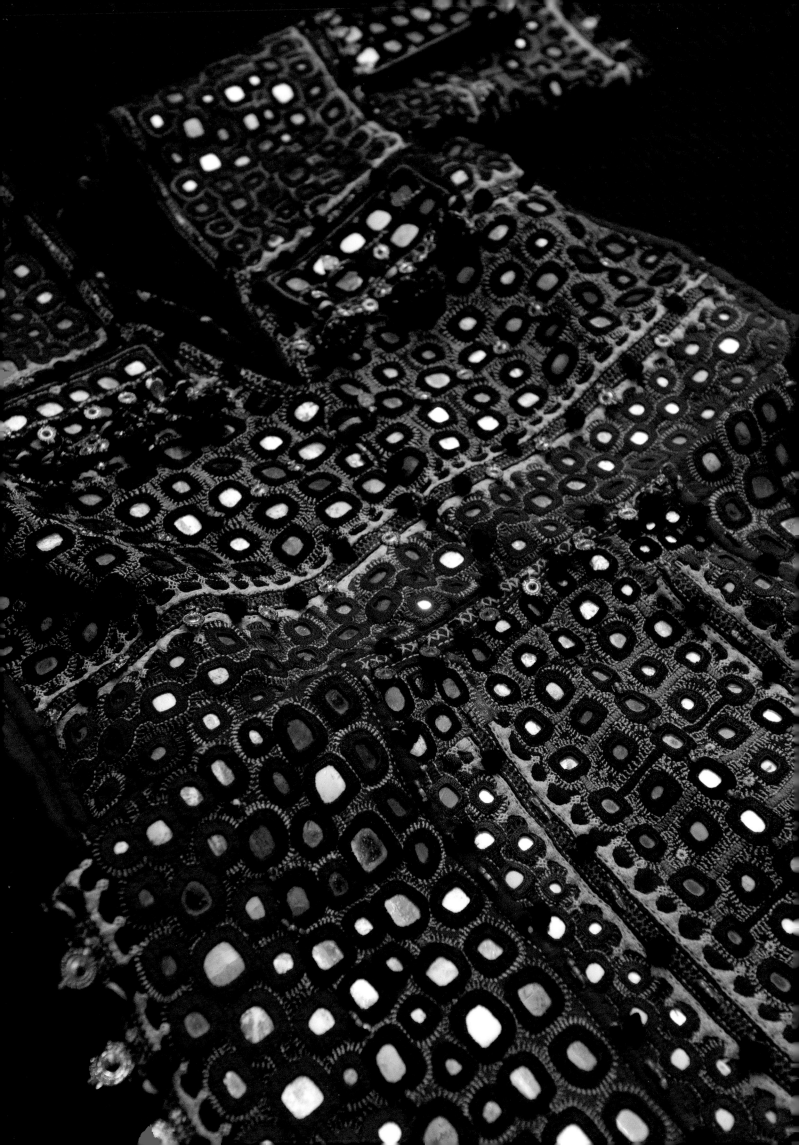

2 HISTORY
Empire of the Caravan

They undertake extensive engagements exporting merchandise, chiefly, grain, cotton, cloths, oil-seeds, etc. and carry them out with the utmost good faith. They never play false once when the work is undertaken by them; no instance has been known of goods entrusted to their care having been robbed. They are looked upon by other classes of natives with suspicious dread, so that they can traverse the wildest and most jungly tracts with impunity and perfect security.

EDWARD BALFOUR, *THE CYCLOPAEDIA OF INDIA*, 1885

FIRST CONTACT

The Greek historian Arrian (1st century CE), writing about Alexander the Great's advance into India, describes a group who led 'a wandering life, dwelling in tents and letting out for hire their beasts of burden.'[1] The reference is vague. It may simply be a description of shepherds. It has, nevertheless, been cited as evidence of established caravan trade and even as the first written description of the Banjara.

Almost a millennia later, the Sanskrit author Dandin composed the *Dashakumaracharita* or *The Tales of the Ten Princes*. It is similar to *One Thousand and One Nights* with much magic and supernatural intervention. In one of the tales, Prince Pramati visits a trader's camp and attends a cockfight. In the camp Pramati meets a Brahmin who helps him attain a woman he met in a dream. The trader's camp is claimed to be a Banjara tanda.[2]

Banjara pre-history has the group located in north-western India, in the desert plains south-east of the Indus river. It is an area that even today is home to many pastoral and semi-nomadic peoples, including the Rabari, Meghwar, Jat and Sodha Rajputs. Embroidery traditions among these groups are still strong and each possesses a set of designs and stitches so distinctive that they can identify who is, and who is not, a member of each tribe. Like a language or a regional accent, clothing and embroidery flag identity. It is not, however, identity as a Westerner might understand it. In the West, each individual articulates a cult of self. Western narratives celebrate the individual rising above the group. In India, on the other hand, community is the prime unit of social organization. The group takes precedence to the point where an individual will answer (with pride) the name of their community when asked who they are. In India, identity means group identity. For the majority of the population, even among members of the same religion, community identity dictates which festivals are observed, if food is raw or cooked, if it is vegetarian or non-vegetarian, who can eat with whom, who can drink with whom, and who can serve or be served.

Tribal culture also dictates marriage rights. A Banjara may only marry another Banjara, so in this respect they are endogamous. But within the tribe, they cannot marry a member of the same family and so at the clan level they are exogamous. These two traits preserve tribal identity and motivate the oral histories of family lineage.

The Banjara might have remained as only another variation among India's north-western tribes were it not for their calling as carriers, an occupation that dispersed their distinctive way of life throughout India. The further away from the tribes of the north-west they moved, the more exceptional they seemed to become. In part, this reputation is due to their reluctance to mingle with other cultures. When passing through another community, the Banjara would always camp outside settlements, hence activating deep notions of order and disorder, romance and prejudice that were equally present in the North American frontier, the medieval European city and India.

> Banjaras are generally thought of as tribals, both by themselves and by others. This view is quite consistent with the Sanskritic concept of sacred and social order as ritually focused in bounded social units. Order belongs to villages and cities, while chaos and disorder characterize the wilderness outside such ritually bounded domains.... Banjaras have traditionally moved in and out of particular social orders without disturbing them and without losing their own cultural integrity.[3]

Brinjarrees on the March, an engraving used to illustrate the 1875 edition of *India and its Native Princes* by Louis Rousselet. 'During the day we witnessed the passage of a caravan of Brinjarrees. Few sights are more picturesque than these caravans on the march, with their thousands of oxen, and their escorts of men of warlike aspect and strangely attired women. The whole family is there; the infant being slung to the back of its mother, and the young children perched on the milking cows, which carry besides all the household utensils.'

Banjara are occasionally referred to as 'Indian Gypsies'. The term 'gypsies' is a difficult one, loaded as it is with stereotypes, misleading information and a long, pejorative history. The term became widespread as it was believed that gypsies originated in Egypt. The idea was spread, at least in part, by groups of Roma as they introduced themselves as displaced or persecuted counts from 'Little Egypt'.[4] Despite the obvious objections to the term, 'gypsy' captures a certain historic context of the Roma, especially their temporary settlement outside of a host community and their hostile reception by most European nations. This prejudice culminated with the Nazi death camps and, sadly, it continues in many forms to the present day.

The appearance of the Banjara, with their headscarves tied back and their singular costume, leads many Westerners who meet them to think they must be 'gypsies'. This impression is often deepened by an offer of fortune telling or some other form of benign sorcery on the beaches of Goa or Mumbai. The question is then posited: are the Banjara gypsies? Because the ancestors of the present-day Roma populations were originally from northern India, the proper formulation for the question would be: are the Roma descended from the Banjara?

Durgibai examining textiles outside her home in Maramanahalli tanda, Karnataka, 2013.

Historic evidence points to the Banjara as camp followers to the Kshattriya (military or warrior cast) located in Rajputana at the turn of the first millennium. The Banjara also claim to be of this caste, a claim supported by those who have observed their martial tendencies. In response to a series of Islamic invasions led by Mahmud of Ghazni (Ghaznivid period 977–1186 CE) an exodus appears to have left India through what is now Afghanistan. Some of the Banjara were no doubt included in this diaspora, if not as the central body, then certainly in the supply train. It seems likely that at the same time Banjara populations also dispersed east to the foothills of the Himalayas and south into Khandesh and Berar or even further to Golconda and Jeypore. Oral histories such as the tale of Prithviraj Chauhan sung by Ramjol Naik Lavudia seem to confirm this general timeline.[5]

The Roma scholar Ian Hancock gives linguistic and historic arguments in support of this hypothesis and further states that the Romani language is a special case of a military camp dialect, or *koïné*, like Urdu, which formed:

> ...from a medley of languages spoken on the battlefields of north-western India. While the speech of those troops who remained in India subsequently normalized in the direction of the surrounding local India languages, those who moved away from the area and became linguistically isolated from it, experienced no such metropolitanizing factor, their speech and linguistic behaviour, as well as their social patterns, developing differently as a result.[6]

Hancock further proposes that such contact languages are not as unusual as one might first suppose. Ghorbati (also Ghorboli, Ghormati, Banjari, Lambhani, etc.), the language spoken by the Banjara among themselves, emerged from the same type of socio-linguistic framework as what he calls *Rajputic*, the *koïné* out of which Romani and Urdu also formed. Conditions in the great Banjara caravans were similar to (and often in support of) military campaigns. The considerable numbers of Banjara who came together and crossed diverse linguistic territory would maintain the conditions of a contact language.

Genetic evidence confirms the linguistic arguments and permits a more accurate assessment of origins. Recent phylogeographical mapping concludes that present-day European Roma populations originated with the 'Doma' or ancient aboriginal populations (including the Banjara) of north-western India.[7]

The first historian's account that mentions caravan trade using pack-bullocks is found during the reign of the Afghan emperor Ala-ud-din Khilji (r. 1296–1316). In an imperial programme of trade control and market regulation, Ala-ud-din licensed merchants and kept profits under state supervision. To extend his control beyond the urban environs he also regulated the grain caravans. Medieval regulations were drastic: the headmen of the communities were put in chains until they agreed to 'bind themselves "like one"' and establish encampments for their 'women and children, oxen and cattle on the banks of the Yamuna, as hostages for their good conduct'. This heavy handed price fixing was just one aspect of running a stable empire. The merchants are referred to as 'karwanis', which literally means 'people of the caravan'. The headman of a group of karwanis is referred to as a naik (nayak) and accounts from 1355 mention that naiks brought food grains into Delhi using trains of 10,000 or 20,000 laden oxen.[8]

Ala-ud-din pursued conquest through what is now Rajasthan and Gujarat and his armies briefly reached the southernmost tip of the Indian peninsula.[9] If he employed Banjara carriers as his supply lines, it is possible that Banjara presence in the south is the result both of an early diaspora and caravan trade.

The formation of one of India's most fantastic artificial lakes is credited to a Banjara tribesman: Pichhu Banjara, who 'built' the Pichola lake of Udaipur in 1362.[10] Four hundred years later, Maharana Jagat Singh II would add a four-acre island in the centre of the water to construct the famous Jag Mandir Palace.

The Muslim chronicler Mahomed Kassim Ferishta, while engaged at the court of Bijapur, recorded how 'in the year 1417 a large convoy of Bunjara bullocks was seized by Khan Khanan...when the former prince rebelled and made an attempt on the throne of Goolburga, the Deccan capital.'[11] The Banjara appear to be already traversing most of southern India at this time, for an account of Vináyaka Deo's founding Jeypore in 1443 mentions that:

Banjara woman wearing a commercially printed light cotton headscarf, Sandur, Karnataka, 2005.

> Not long after his accession, some of his subjects rose against him, but he recovered his position with the help of a leader of Brinjáris; and ever since then, in grateful recognition, his descendents have appended to their signatures a wavy line (called *valatradu*) which represents the rope with which Brinjáris tether their cattle.[12]

Banjara expansion was an effect of successful caravan trade. The historian Irfan Habib has made detailed calculations to determine just how much cargo a pack-bullock could carry, and at what speed the transport became economical:

> Goods were carried on boats and carts and by camels and bullocks. A bullock could travel quite fast, but it would normally be more expensive than a cart. However when the pack-oxen travelled slowly, grazing as they went, and were assembled in herds so as to reduce the cost of watching and guiding them, the expenses of transport were so greatly reduced as to make it the cheapest form possible.[13]

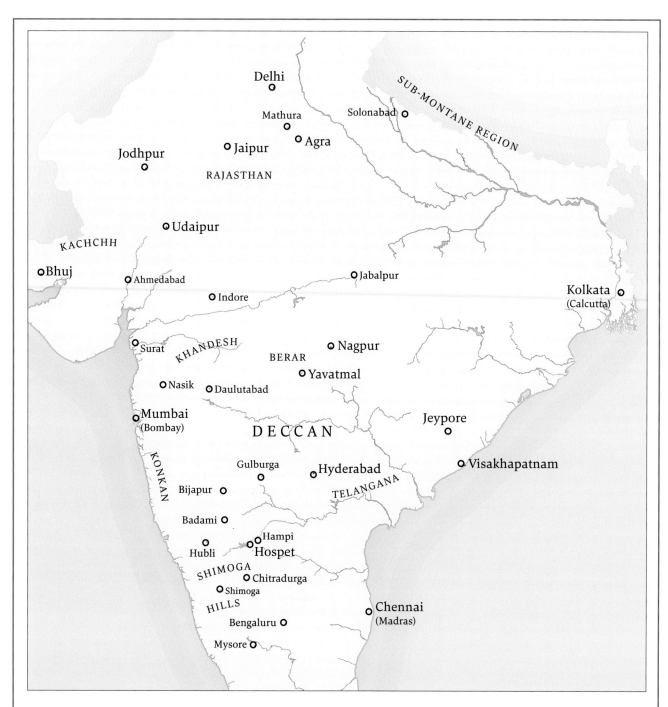

BANJARA: A PEOPLE OF ALL INDIA

Banjara trade routes included bringing salt from both east and west coasts into central India in exchange for grains. They supplied raw cotton to the weaving centres on the east coast between Chennai and Visakhapatnam. In the Khandesh area trade flowed through Indore from Surat and Nasik to Jabalpur. Migrations with oxen through Khandesh to the north Konkan were still recorded as late as the 1960s. The ancestral home of the Banjara is Rajputana (central Rajasthan). From here they dispersed in around 1000 CE.

Military adventures brought them to Gulburga in 1417, and from Delhi they travelled as far north as Kandahar in the early 1600s. Shah Jahan's army brought them to Daulutabad a few decades later. Aurangzeb probably employed them to besiege the Golconda Fort (at Hyderabad) and a century later De Bussy, the French commander, hired them to sneak past besieging armies at Hyderabad. The British engaged them in 1792 as they attacked Sultan Tippu (the Tiger of Mysore) and continued to hire them until the Anglo-

Maratha wars concluded near Surat in 1818. In the north the Banjara occupied much of the sub-montane regions of Nepal and so densely that they resisted the incursions of other settlers and prevented the Mughals from collecting taxes at Solonabad. Their presence in the north remained formidable and as late as 1848 the army contractor Joti Prasad was able to assemble nearly 100,000 Banjara pack-oxen in only three months.

Unlike the more famous caravans of the silk routes, a Banjara caravan carried low-cost, bulky items – usually food grains. They only needed to defend themselves against pilfering. In this regard, they were quite adept. They had little fear that a crack team of bandits on horseback would swoop down and steal their hundred-weight sacks of grain.

With the arrival of the great Mughal emperors, the caravan trade expanded again: both between the growing urban centres and as a supply chain for armed conquest. In his memoirs, Mughal Emperor Jahangir (r. 1605–27) writes how the ox caravans reach a vast size:

> In this country the Banjāras are a fixed class of people, who possess a thousand oxen, or more or less, varying in numbers. They bring grain from the villages to the towns and also accompany armies. With an army...there may at least be a hundred thousand oxen...[14]

One can get a sense of the scale of Banjara operations from Jahangir's observations. The group that he saw were supplying his army on its way from Delhi to Quandahār [Kandahar], a distance of over 1,000 kilometres (600 miles). Jahangir's successor was Shah Jahan (r. 1628–1658), who built the Taj Mahal. His most capable general, Mahabat Khan, set up grain depots and encouraged the Banjara with gifts: 'elephants, horses, and cloths' as well as by fixing the price of grain in the Banjara's favour. His stratagem worked well and when on campaign to the south he 'invested Dowlutabad [a key fortress in western India] so closely with his army that Futteh Khan, the son of Mullic Umbur, was compelled to surrender.' [15]

The Banjara, however, were not always so well disposed toward Mughal royalty. Under the Mughals it was common for rulers to pay debts, or reward loyalty by granting an individual the revenue rights (the *jagir*) to an area. Shortly after coming to power, in a gesture to his own eldest son Prince Dara, Shah Jahan conferred an estate of 148 villages on Dara's wife, Solona. Located in a well-forested, sub-montane region just a few miles south of the present Nepalese border, it was to be Solonabad. 'The attacks of the Banjaras, however, prevented the occupation of the estate, and the jágír was abandoned by the lady...'[16]

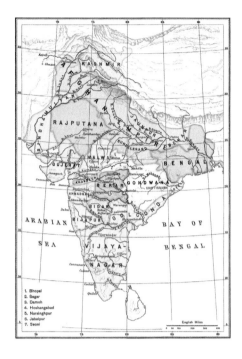

ABOVE
Political map of pre-Mughal India. The Banjara have an ancestral homeland in the Rajputana area. The Banjara language has Rajput, Gujar and Malwa influences.

BELOW
A group of Rajput Banjara living outside of Jaipur. The use of a diaphanous face-covering veil is unusual among the Banjara; who seldom feel the need to place anything between themselves and strangers.

OPPOSITE ABOVE
Bullock-horn ornaments on
embroidered cloth with cowrie
pom-poms and lead pom-
pom collars, Madhya Pradesh,
c. 1940. John Childs collection.

OPPOSITE BELOW
Bullock-horn ornaments on
embroidered cloth with strings
of cowries, Karnataka, *c.* 1940.
Maiwa collection.

BELOW LEFT
The first English map of the
Indian subcontinent. The
original was engraved by
Ronald Elstrack and drafted
by William Baffin. On Thomas
Roe's return voyage to England
on board the *Anne*, Baffin
was the master's mate. Baffin
shared Roe's ambition to map
his journeys. As it stated in the
corner, the map was sold 'in
Paul's Church Yarde by Thomas
Sterne Globemaker'.

BELOW RIGHT
Artwork on the threshold of a
Banjara home in Lambanihalli
tanda, Karnataka. Imagery
of bullocks still figures
prominently in Banjara culture.

It was during the height of the Mughal empire that Europeans first began to gather on the coastlines, seeking permission to construct warehouses (termed factories) in port towns. Although Queen Elizabeth I famously granted her charter to what was to become the East India Company at the close of the year 1600, the British did not reach the shores of India until 24 August 1608. The company was initially more interested in the highly profitable trade (and piracy) that could be conducted in South-East Asia. Nevertheless, in 1615 the English Ambassador Thomas Roe arrived in Surat on India's western coast and began to make his way towards the capital. He hoped to meet with Jahangir and negotiate permission to build a factory in Surat. While travelling through Khandesh, Roe describes how 'I mett in one day 10,000 bullocks in one troupe laden with corne, and most days others, but lesse; which shows the pleanty.'[17]

Roe was permitted his factory and thirteen years later, in 1628, the Cornish merchant-adventurer Peter Mundy left London and arrived in Surat. He was a keen observer and kept a journal of his travels. He also occasionally sketched. Mundy followed a similar route to Roe and on 23 August 1632 he records his encounter with one of the fabled pack-ox trains: 'In the morninge wee mett a Tanda or Banjara of Oxen, in number 14,000, all layden with graine, as wheat, rice, etts.'[18] Mundy proceeds to calculate the capacity of each ox and relates how he had seen many such caravans as they made their way to Agra.

> Theis Banjares carrie all their howsehold alonge with them, as wives and children, one Tanda consisting of many families.... Their Oxen are their owne. They are sometymes hired by Marchants, but most commonly they are the Marchants themselves, buyinge of graine where it is Cheape to be had, and carryeinge it to places where it is dearer, and from thence againe relade themselves with any thinge that will yeild benefitt in other places, as Salt, Sugar, Butter, etts.[19]

Mundy's observations make a number of important points: the Banjara prefer to work as independent merchants, not hired labour. They own animals individually,

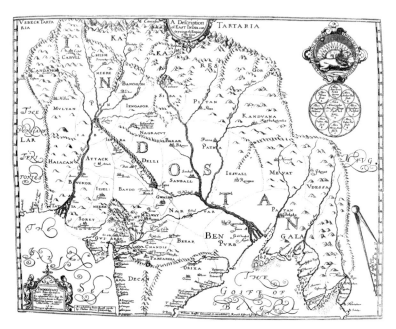

but they negotiate work as a collective. The word 'tanda' identifies both the family group and the encampment.

> There may bee in such a Tanda 6 or 700 persons, men, weomen and Children. There Men are very lustie, there weomen hardie, whoe in occasion of fight, lay about them like men. Theis people goe dispersedly, driveing their Laden Oxen before them, their Journey not above 6 or 7 miles a daye att most, and that in the Coole. When they have unladen their Oxen, they turne them a graizeinge, heere being ground enough, and noe man to forbidd them.[20]

Two days later, Mundy met a train of oxen carrying sugar. It was raining and the goods were unloaded and covered with tents. When asked how many oxen there were, the carriers replied: '20,000'.

The English were not the only travellers on the sea. The son of a French geographer and map dealer, Jean-Baptiste Tavernier, financed his own voyages to satisfy his wanderlust and his merchant ambitions. During his second voyage (1638–43) he visited Agra and met Jahangir's son, the Emperor Shah Jahan. Tavernier also travelled further south to the Deccan and the Golconda kingdom (near present-day Hyderabad) where he visited India's fabled diamond mines. It was in this region that he acquired the legendary (and perhaps cursed) Great Blue Diamond, also known as Tavernier's Blue, which was later recut and renamed the Hope Diamond.

Tavernier compiled records of his journeys with the help of at least two literary assistants: Samuel Chappuzeau and André Daulier-Deslandes. The work, first published in 1676, was immensely popular and satisfied a public hungry for tales of foreign lands. Hasty translations were prepared and in 1677 the first English version appeared. Oddly for a work of travel writing, Tavernier's account is not chronological: rather it is largely anecdotal, collecting experiences from many years and grouping them together loosely by subject.[21]

Tavernier sets out the modes of transport used in seventeenth-century India. He details how much an elephant can carry and at what speeds; how many men are required and what to pay to transport an individual by palanquin; and how 'it is an astonishing sight to behold caravans numbering 10,000 or 12,000 oxen together, for the transport of rice, corn, and salt.'

ABOVE
Jean-Baptiste Tavernier shown wearing robes of honour presented to him by the Shah of Persia.

OPPOSITE
Above: Decorations for the face of an ox, Hyderabad region, *c.* 1970. John Childs collection. Below: Decoration for the face of an ox, *c.* 1960. Maiwa collection.

BELOW
Modes of carrying in India used to illustrate the 1875 edition of *India and its Native Princes* by Louis Rousselet. This oxen carries a water skin with a spout at the bottom.

When the season presses, and they wish to have the goods quickly at Surat, in order to ship them, they load them on oxen, and not on carts. As all the territories of the Great Mogul are well cultivated, the fields are enclosed by good ditches, and each has its tank or reservoir for irrigation. This it is which is so inconvenient for travellers, because, when they meet caravans of this description in narrow roads, they are sometimes obliged to wait two or three days till all have passed. Those who drive these oxen follow no other trade all their lives; they never dwell in houses, and they take with them their women and children. Some of them posses 100 oxen, other have more or fewer, and they all have a Chief, who acts as a prince, and who always has a chain of pearls suspended from his neck. When the caravan which carries corn and that which carries rice meet, rather than give way, one to the other, they often engage in very sanguinary encounters. The Great Mogul, considering one day that these quarrels were prejudicial to commerce and to the transport of food in his kingdom, arranged that the Chiefs of the two caravans should come to see him. When they arrived, the King, after he had advised them for their mutual benefit to live for the future in harmony with each other, and not to fight anymore when they met, presented each of them with a lākh, or 100,000 rupees and a chain of pearls.[22]

Tavernier refers to the pack carriers as 'manaris', which appears to be a confusion with the name of a pedlar caste.[23] He also gives a strange description of the salt carriers, claiming they may be identified by 'a lump of salt, suspended from the neck in a bag, which weighs sometimes from 8 to 10 livres [between 8 and 10 pounds] (for the heavier it is the more honour they have in carrying it).' If true, it would explain the Banjara affection for heavy ornaments. Of the women he writes:

> The dress of the women is but simple cloth white or coloured which is bound five or six times like a petticoat from the waist downwards, as if they had three or four, one above the other. From the waist upwards they tattoo their skin with flowers, as when one applies cupping glasses, and they paint these flowers divers colours with the juice of roots, in such a manner that it seems as though their skin was a flowered fabric.[24]

Following closely behind Tavernier was the German adventurer Johan Albrecht de Mandelslo, who, after completing his diplomatic mission to Isfahan, proceeded to India where he followed the usual tourist trail for foreign visitors. He landed in Surat and passed through Ahmedabad on his way to Agra. On his way he encountered the Banjara. Like Mundy, he observed that the caravan was a moving camp with women and children, he confirmed that they were independent merchants and, like Mundy, he commented on the martial qualities of the women:

> There are a certain sort of People call'd Venesers in Decan, whose chief business is to buy up vast quantities of Wheat and Rice here, and to carry it in great Caravans of 1000 Beasts at a time, to Indosthan and other Neighbouring Countries; they carry their Families along with them, their Wives being so expert and brave in managing of the Bow, that they serve them for a Guard against the Rasboutes [Rajputs] and other Robbers.[25]

ABOVE
Pack-bullock and driver,
pen and ink wash, *c.* 1810,
by George Chinnery.

OPPOSITE
Renavva and ox near Badami,
Karnataka, 2013. Oxen are
still used throughout India
for agriculture, however,
they are seldom outfitted
as pack-bullocks. Most oxen
are harnessed as teams.

During their campaigns into the Deccan, the Mughal armies made good use of the Banjara as a commissariat force. Capable, strong and with a hereditary ability to endure the gruelling life of long-distance carriage, the Banjara were the obvious choice. The caravan empires were to expand again under the constant campaigning of India's most shrewd military strategist and ambitious monarch: Aurangzeb. From 1658, the year he seized power, until he was an octogenarian in 1705, Aurangzeb worked tirelessly to expand his empire and consolidate territory. As a militant ruler who never stopped campaigning, he had a vested interest in the location of the Banjara hordes. In a letter from the last years of his reign, Aurangzeb observed that large numbers of the Banjara had gone to Gujarat, but, failing to find sufficient grains to trade, they had loaded their bullocks with salt and dispersed to other parts. 'Yet Banjaras with "a hundred thousand oxen" still remained in that province trying to buy grain and return to the Deccan across the Narbada.'[26]

He was a brilliant general in command of vast resources and yet Aurangzeb could not establish permanent control of the Deccan. He spent the last twenty-six years of his life trying to stamp out the brush fires of insurrection that repeatedly sparked up across his southern conquests. The conditions in Aurangzeb's mobile military camp were such that, amazingly, 100,000 pack-bullocks do not seem very much.

> [Aurangzeb's] moving capital alone – a city of tents thirty miles in circumference, some two hundred and fifty bazaars, with half a million camp followers, fifty thousand camels, and thirty thousand elephants, all of whom had to be fed, stripped peninsular India of any and all of its surplus grain and wealth through the quarter century of its intrusion.[27]

In the end, even Aurangzeb gave in to despair and turned his back on the ceaseless battles, waste and carnage. 'I came alone and I go a stranger. I do not know who I am, nor what I have been doing. The instant which has passed in power has left only sorrow behind it.' So did a dying Aurangzeb confess to his son in February 1707. 'I have sinned terribly, and I do not know what punishment awaits me.'[28] He died on a Friday (an Islamic holy day) and was buried at Khuldabad, in a small austere tomb without ornament.

OPPOSITE
Younger women like Chandrammabai often combine traditional and modern clothing, varying the mix to suit their taste and the occasion. Photographed in Sandur, Karnataka, 2005.

BELOW
A *pachela* (armlet) with cowrie florets, lead beads, bells, coins and an embroidered cloth band. Such armlets are an essential part of traditional dress and vital for participation in any Banjara dance, *c.* 1930. Maiwa collection.

With the death of Aurangzeb, the empire shattered and rival forces fought over the pieces. Groups of Banjara would hire themselves to all contenders. The Marathas expanded into central and southern India and the Nizam of Hyderabad quietly slipped out from under the yoke of Mughal rule to become an independent ruler. European interests began their incursions with the English establishing bases in Calcutta, Bombay and Madras (known as Kolkata, Mumbai and Chennai today), and the French securing a fortified port at Pondicherry.

In the complex power politics of the Deccan, the French proved themselves adept at backing key contenders and manipulating loyalties. When the newly independent Nizam-ul-Mulk of Hyderabad died, for example, the French made substantial gains in revenue and territory by exploiting the succession rivalry. The gains were due in no small part to the genius of commander Marquis de Bussy-Castelnau. Even when besieged (as he was in August 1756, in the gardens of Charmaul, near Hyderabad), De Bussy managed to have a supply of beef and almost everything else he could want. He was supplied, of course, by the Banjara traders. The historian Robert Orme writes:

> [T]he army at Charmaul was constantly supplied with cattle for the shambles, and forage for the horses, oxen, camels, and elephants, by bands of a people called Lamballis, peculiar to the Deccan, who are continually moving up and down the country with their flocks, and contract to furnish the armies in the field.[29]

Orme then remarks, as many others have, that the Banjara were neutral: each side suffered them to supply the opposition during a conflict. A siege was naturally a different matter, but money in the right hands could overcome this also:

> The union amongst all these bands renders each respectable even to the enemy of the army they are supplying; but they are not permitted to deal with places besieged; nevertheless Mr. Bussy surmounted this objection by bribing the Morrattoes [Marathas], who, for the sake of marauding, undertook the patroles of Salabadjing's army, to let the Lamballis pass in the night...[30]

Marquis de Bussy survived the siege, and eventually his enemies sued for peace. French power in the Deccan, however, was distracted by events back in Europe. Thirty years later it would be the ambitious British who were courting the Banjara.

A BRITISH ROMANCE

Of the many young men working for the East India Company in the capacity of clerks, or 'writers', surely the most prolific was John Forbes. A skilled draughtsman with an eye for natural history, Forbes filled 150 folio volumes (52,000 pages) with his drawings, observations and notes.[31] Towards the end of his time in India he had risen to the position of Collector for the Baroche district (located just north of Surat). In January 1783 he made a tour with 'five English gentlemen' travelling in the style of Mughal royalty. They used two sets of tents. While they used the first set, servants went ahead to set up a second camp, getting everything ready for the gentlemen. Like other travellers he 'met with large caravans of banjarrees' who

A Foot Soldier in the Usual Costume of the Native Indians by James Forbes. The original illustration was made by Forbes in 1775 and an engraving of the illustration was included in the second publication of Forbes's memoirs in 1823.

'do not belong to any particular country.' Forbes observes a wide variety of goods being carried, indicating the expanding influence of European trade:

> These people travel from interior towns to the sea coast, with caravans of oxen, sometimes consisting of several thousand, laden with corn, oil, and manufactured goods of cotton and silk. They return with raw cotton, spices, woollen cloths, iron, copper, and other articles imported from Europe, and distant parts of Asia: the greatest number are laden with salt, which finds a ready sale in every habitable spot, from the sea to the summit of the Ghaut mountains.[32]

Like his illustrations, Forbes's prose communicates a wealth of detail and nuance. He is most impressed with the epic scale of the caravan journeys. As Forbes was himself engaged in a game of camp leap-frog, he pays particular attention to the way the Banjara move their tandas.

> The vanjarrahs from distant countries seldom make more than one annual journey to commute their merchandize at the seaports; travelling with their wives and children in the patriarchal style, they seem a happy set of people.... A hundred fires are often blazing together in their camp, where the women prepare curry, pilaw, or some savoury dish, to eat with the rice and dholl.... Some of these merchants travel fifteen hundred or two thousand miles during the fair season; and, as they make only one journey, they contrive to give it every possible advantage. For this purpose each bullock carries a double load, which they effect in this manner: moving on one stage with their loaded oxen, wives and children, they fix upon a shady spot, to unload the cattle; leaving the family and merchandize under the care of a guard, they drive back the empty oxen for a second load; which is brought forwards, and deposited in their tents. The cattle having rested, move on to the next station, with the first packages; returning empty, they proceed again with the second load, and thus continue a trading journey, throughout the whole fair season.[33]

Forbes is also the British Collector for the district, hence he has an equally enthusiastic interest in why the Banjara are not harassed during transport....

> The vanjarrahs are protected by all governments, pay the stated duties at the frontier passes, and are never molested. For further security, a bhaut generally accompanies the caravan; the bhauts or churrons are a caste feared and respected by all the Hindoo tribes; an old woman of that description is a sufficient protection for a whole caravan. If plundered, or ill treated, without reparation, either the protecting bhaut, or one of the tribe, sheds his blood in the presence of the aggressors; a dreadful deed, supposed to be always followed by divine vengeance. The vanjarrahs are likewise followed by conjurors, astrologers, jugglers, musicians, dancing bears, dancing-snakes, monkeys, and various entertainments; they gain a livelihood by what they receive in the camp, or pick up in the towns and villages through which they pass.[34]

TOP
Anklets worn by women living near Maheshwar, Madhya Pradesh, 2014.

ABOVE
Double anklets worn by women living near Devarakonda, Telangana, 2004. 'A criminal in irons would not have much more to incommode him than these damsels deem ornamental and agreeable.'

The Banjara are (largely) left alone because the *bhaut* (a bard, oral historian, genealogist storyteller, and shaman, all in one) is considered sacred. In what seems a fantastic defence strategy, the *bhauts* would kill themselves rather than have property stolen – thus haunting the thieves with a supernatural vengeance. The security of the *bhaut* was more effective in Hindu populations who shared the superstition, less so with Muslims. Forbes's account is an evocative description of peace-time trade. British expansion in southern India would soon necessitate a need to hire the Banjara in a military capacity.

In 1791, the 20-year-old Edward Moor was in command of a grenadier company about to attack the forces of Tipu Sultan. He had departed from England at the very young age of 11 for a career with the East India Company. Moor possessed a quick intelligence and a gift for Indian languages. He was also a keen observer, fascinated by the cultures of the Indian States. He had become lieutenant by the age of 17, and in June 1791 he was wounded while leading an assault on the hill fort at Doridroog, near Bangalore. It was now December and he was about to be wounded again.[35]

The East India Company was engaged in its third war (1791–92) with the Kingdom of Mysore. Tipu Sultan was an enlightened leader, whose use of innovative military tactics (he deployed iron-cased rockets) was matched only by his hatred of the English. Against Tipu, Moor was serving under Captain John Little in a British force joined by some 30,000 Marathas.

The two additional wounds that Moor would receive put him out of action and forced a return home to England on sick leave. It was during this convalescence that he wrote his first major work. *A Narrative of the Operations of Captain Little's Detachment* was published in 1794.

Moor first met the Banjara while he was still a teenager. He was no romantic, but still he was fascinated.

> Grain, which until this time had continued exorbitantly dear, now lowered in price, as considerable quantities were brought from the northward by the Bandjarrahs, of which people what little we have remarked shall here be given.

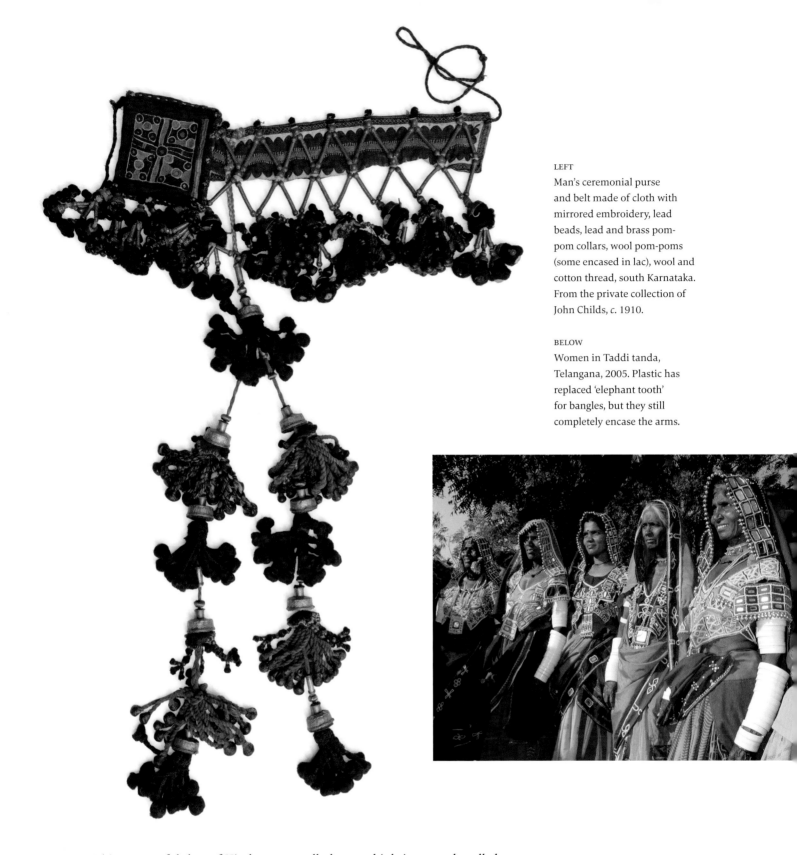

This very useful class of Hindoos, generally, but we think, improperly, called Brinjarries, have customs and manners peculiar to themselves; it is not however in our power to give any satisfactory particulars concerning them. They associate chiefly together, seldom or never mixing with other tribes; they seem to have no home, nor character, but that of merchants, in which capacity they travel great distances to whatever parts are most in want of their merchandise, which is the greatest part corn. In times of war they attend, and are of great assistance to armies, and, being neutral, it is a matter of indifference to them who purchase their goods.[36]

Moor confirms that the larger Banjara camps (tandas) were a considerable military force. They undertook their own defence and could be counted on to protect their cargo from petty raids or the incursions of enemy foragers. They remained apart and did not mingle with either the local residents or the military camps:

> We observed the Bandjarrahs seldom, either on the march or in camp mixed at all with the Bhow's army, but marched and formed their own encampments apart, relying on their own courage for protection, for which purpose the men are all armed with swords or matchlocks.[37]

It was not just the aloof nature of the Banjara camps that drew attention, however, it was the women that elicited the most curiosity:

> The women drive the cattle, and are the most robust we ever saw in India, undergoing a great deal of labour with apparent ease; their dress is peculiar, and their ornaments so singularly chosen that we have, we are confident, seen women who (not to mention a child at their backs) have had eight or ten pounds weight in metal or ivory round their arms and legs. The favourite ornaments appear to be rings of ivory from the wrist to the shoulder, regularly increasing in size, so that the ring near the shoulder will be immoderately large, sixteen or eighteen inches, or more perhaps in circumference. These rings are sometimes dyed red. Silver, lead, copper, or brass, in ponderous bars, encircle their shins, sometimes round, others in the form of festoons, and truly we have seen some so circumstanced that a criminal in irons would not have much more to incommode him than these damsels deem ornamental and agreeable trappings on a long march, for they are never dispensed with in the hottest weather.[38]

LEFT
Ceremonial coverings for the tip of a spear, embroidered cloth, cowries, lead beads and cord, Karnataka, c. 1900. Left: Maiwa collection. Right: John Childs collection.

OPPOSITE
Banjara elders near Badami, Karnataka, 2013.

Political map of India, *c.* 1900. Seringapatam is immediately north of Mysore. The pink areas of the map are directly administered by the British. Yellow areas are 'princely states' administered by Rajas sympathetic to British interests. The Madras Presidency is on the east coast, the Bombay Presidency is on the west and Goa, a Portuguese territory, is white.

The observation is still accurate. Contemporary Banjara women who prefer traditional dress are remarkable for the sheer weight of ornament that they consider desirable. The anklets, in particular, remain substantial and inordinately heavy. Moor goes on to describe the woman's dress in detail:

> A kind of stomacher, with holes for the arms, and tied behind at the bottom, covers the breast, and has some strings of cowries, depending behind, dangling at their backs. The stomacher is curiously studded with cowries, and their hair is also bedecked with them. They wear likewise ear-rings, necklaces, rings on the fingers and toes, and, we think, the nut or nose jewel. In contra-distinction to most eastern females, the Hindoos in particular, the Bandjarras pay little or no regard to cleanliness; their hair, once plaited, is not combed or opened perhaps for a month; their bodies or cloaths are seldom washed; their arms indeed are so encased with ivory, that it would be no easy matter to clean them.[39]

Again, what is unusual in this description is how easily it could be applied to contemporary Banjara. Moor's observations were made in 1791 or earlier. At the time Lord Cornwallis was Governor General and commander-in-chief of India. To give the date some perspective, only a decade earlier Cornwallis had been forced to surrender at Yorktown during the American War of Independence. Moor goes on to compare the men and women, and to remark on what everyone found astonishing: the size of the bullock trains.

They [the women] are chaste and affable; any indecorum offered to a woman would be resented by the men, who have a high sense of honour on that head, and are said in general to be honourable in their dealings; they seem to be somewhat reserved and grave. Some of them are men of great property; it is said that droves of loaded bullocks, to the number of fifty or sixty thousand, have at different times followed the Bhow's army; and two days before we last crossed the Toombudra, Mr. Twiss informed us a drove passed light from Appah Sahib's army consisting, he was assured, of eighty thousand. The men, although in general well knit, are not to appearance robust in proportion to the women: the latter are by no means handsome; we never saw more than two or three who would, even with the aid of clean linen (an advantageous point of view, by the way in which we never saw one) have been reckoned attractive.[40]

Despite his opinions on female beauty, Moor was a sympathetic observer – both to the Banjara specifically and Indian culture generally. After his convalescence in England he returned to India but his health did not last. In 1805, at the age of only 35, Moor was invalided home. Back in England he began work on his major publication, *The Hindu Pantheon*, an introduction to Hinduism for an English readership. The work marked a period of orientalism by British scholars who were anxious to understand Indian civilization (as far as possible) on its own terms. They did not seek to belittle it, replace it, or redefine it to serve colonial aims. In contrast, an India that was seen as the wellspring of despotic rulers and heathen gods became the increasingly strident characterization that served to justify British hegemony and missionary zeal.

Of a like mind to Moor was Mark Wilks, who was 33 when he took part in the Third Anglo-Mysore War. A future cartographer and capable historian, Wilks gave a detailed account of how the British contracted the Banjara as an independent, self-contained commissariat force.

Much has been conjectured, and little ascertained regarding this extraordinary class of men, whose habits and history were at that period entirely unknown to the English Army. Every man and many of the women were armed with a great variety of weapons and although moving with their whole train of women and children, who could scarcely be classed among the impediments, proved themselves capable, in several instances, not only of military defence, but of military enterprise, as was particularly evinced in the assault and plunder of the lower fort of Cabal Droog. Farther they are known by the name of Brinjaries, a supposed Persian compound, designating their office with an army; in the south they are called Lumbanies, but no conjecture has been hazarded regarding this name, and they have not even a tradition regarding their origin. After a discussion of some length with an assembly of chiefs regarding their descent, and pressing for some traditional account of their original country or home, 'That is our country,' said the eldest among them, pointing to the tent which covered his grain bags, 'and wherever it is pitched is our home, my ancestors never told me of any other;' and nothing can be added of fact or conjecture except that their language is northern, and apparently a dialect of the Peuj-aub-ee. [Punjabi][41]

Diagram of a pack-bullock with gear for carriage, from *Military Transport* (1882), a British military manual by Lieut.-Col. George Armand Furse. Furse claims that 'what is used in the Madras Presidency, and in the Sagor and Jubbulpore districts, are about the best.' In addition to the pads pictured, pack-oxen used a *salleetah*. 'Salleetahs are large pieces of strong gunny or coarse canvas furnished all round with eyelet holes or loops through which is passed a rope; when this rope is drawn tight the canvas assumes the form of a bag. These contrivances are especially useful for carrying miscellaneous articles and form part of the gear of all pack transport animals in India.'

'They have great skill in driving cattle, four men managing a hundred bullocks. They say that by their shouts they can make the bullocks charge and overrun a tiger or a small body of men. When they halt they surround their camp with a pile of sacks, musket-proof and too high for a horse to jump.' *Gazetteer of the Bombay Presidency, Khandesh District.* 1880.

To engage the merchants, the British would advance both money and 'certificates' to the naiks. The certificates permitted the Banjara to purchase grain in areas under British control. They brought the grain back and were permitted to sell it in the military camp at market rates. They then repaid the advance and, if needed, repeated the process. The natural inclination of the Banjara to keep to themselves was perceived as neutrality when dealing with armies. Many accounts mention their ability to work for either side and Wilks notes that the supply train that arrived on 23 January 1792 reached 60,000 pack-bullocks. 'Many of them formerly attendant on the house of Hyder' [Hyder Ali, the father of Tipu Sultan].

Eighteenth-century India was in a state of almost continual warfare with the British and French as relative newcomers to conflicts between Marathas, Rajputs, Mughals and the Hyderabad Nizam. In addition, there were wars of succession when a powerful ruler died and the heirs and their armies squared off against each other. In the Third Anglo-Mysore War, Wilks estimated that 'the number of strangers in Mysore in the campaign of 1792 could not have fallen below 400,000.' Even without the predation, looting and scorched-earth tactics of the conflicts, such populations quickly exhausted local food supplies. The ability of an army on the move to access distant stores was paramount. The Banjara were courted by shrewd military commanders:

It was the obvious purpose of Lord Cornwallis that grain should be plenty, not cheap, for cheapness would check the inducements of the merchant, and diminish the supply; while therefore no limitation in price was attempted, he always assured the merchant a fair profit, by purchasing on the public account whenever it fell below a certain standard and dispatching the adventurers for a fresh cargo, and by steady adherence to these simple commercial principals he assured an abundance which had never before been experienced in an English campaign.[42]

If, when the grains arrived at the military camp, the price was low, the Banjara would hold onto the grains, waiting for supply to drop and prices to increase. If there was a great demand and prices were high they would sell immediately. These ambitions matched exactly those of the military commanders 'to be as speedily supplied as he can when it is scarce; and not to overstock the market in times of plenty.'

Although the mutually beneficial economics certainly motivated the Banjara to supply British camps preferentially, Banjara neutrality could be seen as problematic. The advance of capital and the certificates (necessary for purchase of such large amounts of grain from allied territories) were a British innovation and an attempt to indenture the merchants. Six years after the conclusion of the Third Anglo-Mysore War, the British once again drew battle lines against the

A group of Banjara women assembled in the centre of Kadiyala Kunta tanda. In this area, necklaces made from strings of small white beads are very popular. The bags display a motif similar to those found in Banjara embroidery and are a source of pride, Kadiyala Kunta tanda, 2014.

Tiger of Mysore, Tipu Sultan. The siege of Seringapatam was to test the free market theories of the Banjara–British relationship.

In this conflict, the Resident at Hyderabad, James Kirkpatrick (the main character in William Dalrymple's *White Mughals*) 'advanced 150,000 rupees to the [Banjara] chief at Hyderabad, and there were mustered below the Ghauts 25,000 bullock-loads of grain.'[43]

At the siege of Seringapatam grain supplies were blocked by enemy forces until an armed escort could be sent to guide them through. The merchants arrived late, a few days after Seringapatam fell. However, Tipu's river island fortress was so well stocked with grain that the price dropped to 2 per cent of what the previously distressed troops had been paying.

> [I]f the British general had adhered to the letter of the compact with the Banjaras they must have been ruined, and it is more than likely they would never have joined us again; but that liberality which distinguishes our government from all others in the East compromised the matter, and secured the hearty co-operation and assistance of these useful people in a subsequent war with the Murhuttas. The whole of the grain was purchased at the average rate of five seers for a rupee; the Banjaras returned the original sum advanced to them and had sufficient remaining to pay them for their labour, expense, and risk. The chief naiqs received honorary dresses and swords, and their leader Bheema Bhungy was presented with an elephant.[44]

It is at this point that the encouragement of Banjara fidelity becomes a matter of concern to the highest levels of the East India Company. Records by the Board of Commissioners for the Affairs of India (1798–99) show a clear desire to entice the merchants to settle within the Company's territories. 'When it is considered how helpless an army is without numerous attendants of this description, the [indispensability of them to] a constant state of preparedness is obvious.' The Company is hopeful that settlement will solve the largest difficulty in dealing with the Banjara: delay.

> [N]either the difficulty or the delay originates with the Brinjarries who are ready enough to join our camp, where they are certain of good treatment and handsome profit, but in the managers of the countries where they reside and through which they have to pass, who always take advantage of them to extract heavy duties, and who have it in their power whenever policy dictates to prevent this class of men attending the summons of Government.[45]

Supplying the constant warfare in southern India had made the Banjara both wealthy and powerful. Yet the British observe the carriers being delayed and excessively taxed. If the Banjara suffered exploitation at this time, when they enjoyed substantial military backing, it did not auger well: the notes of the Board of Commissioners contain a dark foreshadowing of the Banjara's future. The records also demonstrate a certain naïveté in dealing with the group, anticipating that they will be easily settled:

Large quilted bag, embroidered with running stitch, brick stitch, cross stitch, cretan stitch and buttonhole stitch, 74 × 48 cm, Madhya Pradesh, *c.* 1960. Maiwa collection.

Lord Cornwallis, fully sensible of the benefits to be expected from having some of this class of Men as inhabitants, directed Lieutenant Colonel Read to give... the head Banjarrie who attended the army to Seringapatam, a tract in the Baramahal on easy terms, both as a reward for his past services and as a security for the future. This plan as I understand, succeeded to the fullest of his wishes, and proves beyond a doubt that similar encouragement would induce the settlement of this Cast throughout the Company's territories...[46]

Expectations were high, but the bribe was ultimately unsuccessful.

A third name may be added to the list of orientalist chroniclers writing about the Banjara: John Briggs. He shared many qualities with Moor and Wilks, including fluency with languages and an early start in India. During 1812 he was the Persian Interpreter to the Officer commanding the Hyderabad Subsidiary Force. Stationed at Jaulna, and 'The amount of Persian interpreting that was required being very limited', he was soon employed in the 'carriage and intelligence department.' This brought him into direct contact with the Banjara merchants and he compiled as much information as he could from first-hand sources; 'the materials being gathered entirely from my conversations with them, and inquiries as to their traditions and customs.'[47] The Banjara might have enjoyed a better future had Briggs's account made its way into more high-level official circles, but it was

A large ceremonial quilt with cotton threads on cotton fabric, backed with block-printed cotton. The composition is deliberately asymmetric: one corner element is omitted and the red circle in the lower right is placed in such a way as to appear almost random, 95 × 95 cm, Madhya Pradesh, c. 1910. Maiwa collection.

published in the *Transactions of the Literary Society of Bombay*. It was largely left to others with far less direct knowledge to shape opinion on the itinerant traders.

An alternative to the English system of working with the Banjara was taken by the Maratha freebooter Dhoondiah Vagh, who employed them almost as privateers. Languishing in prison at the fall of Seringapatam he either escaped or was set free. Vagh was a raider who maintained his power through 'threats, intimidation, and the imaginative use of dense terrain'.[48] His pillage was troublesome, however, it seems it was his move to reunite a considerable number of Tipu Sultan's disbanded troops that led the British and, in particular Arthur Wellesley, the future Duke of Wellington, to pursue him. In a dispatch sent on 7 September 1800, three days before defeating Dhoondiah Vagh, Wellesley writes that he had 'got a tandah of above 10,000 brinjarries', which he immediately commissioned.

> These brinjarries give a curious account of the manner in which Dhoondiah goes on. They say that he has with him still above 40,000 of their class that he employs them and gives them the means of living in the following manner. When he approaches a village or a town which is unprotected by a fort, he sends a body of horse, and of brinjarries to levy a contribution; he takes to himself all the money he can get, and gives them at a certain low price all the grain and all the cattle they can find. They pay him this price for the grain and cattle and they are allowed to sell them at such profit as his camp will afford.[49]

When the British advanced funds to the Banjara for supplies the free market rhetoric evaporated. Supplies purchased on the British account could only arrive at the British camps. Colonel Dalrymple encountered a group of Banjara 'in the employ of the British government' who were attempting to 'go over' to Dhoondiah Vagh. Dalrymple 'by way of example to those accompanying him, hung seven of the principal niaqs, and explained to them that our vengeance was not less to be dreaded than our liberality was to be desired.'[50]

During the Second Anglo-Maratha War (1803–05) Briggs observed that the British success depended on the ability of the Banjara community to deliver grains and stores economically in the vast quantities needed. 'It was in consequence of this admirable system that the army was enabled to move with facility and celerity in every direction.' The numbers of bullocks grew as the British took over more and more territory and in August 1803, 84,000 were mustered in the camp of Colonel Stevenson.[51]

Man's ceremonial belt, embroidered cloth, lead beads, lead pom-pom collars, pom-poms, mirrors and cord, *c.* 1930. Maiwa collection.

Dhani Kethavath crossing the road. The *peti* in her *kachali* is quite narrow, a detail that identifies blouses made in the Hyderabad region. Photographed in Davarsella tanda, Telangana, 2014.

Briggs, a consummate story-teller, relates a second more curious instance of a small tanda going over to the enemy. They were intercepted by an officer named Dooly Khan in command of a group of the Nizam's cavalry. Wellesley wrote to Dooly Khan to seize the grain and hang the naik. The officer appropriated the grain but did not execute the leader. Several years later, in 1808, the same naik, finding himself negotiating for stores, complained that a large quantity of grain had been seized by Dooly Khan without payment. The matter went to the Hyderabad Resident, Thomas Sydenham, who was requested to recover the money from Dooly Khan. Sydenham arranged a meeting with Khan and the naik but did not inform either of them about the subject of the meeting:

After being seated the subject was introduced, and the Bunjara naik called in. Dooly Khan instantly recollected the circumstance, and said, 'I have got about me the order to hang that old man'; and produced, from among a number of other letters which he took out of his turban, the identical letter.[52]

Captain Sydenham congratulated the naik on his considerable good fortune and he was released unharmed. Apparently out of admiration for Wellesley, Dooly Khan kept every letter sent to him, convinced that they were a talisman and so long as they were on his person, they would protect him from harm.

Wellesley, for his part, seems to have experienced a mounting frustration with the Banjara merchants. As British territory grew and his own responsibilities increased, the dependence on an autonomous community for crucial supply trains must have seemed unwise. Ultimately, the goals of imperial empire building were not those of the Banjara – especially when monsoons or disease led to large losses of oxen.[53]

Neither were the Banjara always happy to move at the rate the British forces desired. When the British first engaged the Banjara in 1791, a native commissary would accompany the group.[54] The role of this person was more actuarial than martial, however, they were often charged with encouraging the Banjara to move faster. In a dispatch of 8 June 1803 to J. H. Piele, Secretary to the Resident at Mysore, Wellesley laments:

> The sepoys are sent with each party, in order to urge them forward, and to prevent them from doing mischief in the country through which they pass. It frequently happens, as it has in the instance to which you have alluded, that the sepoys are of no use, and their presence deters the country magistrates from interfering, and keeping the brinjarries in order. But sometimes the brinjarries will not attend to the sepoys, and even beat them; as a party did lately some of my sepoys who urged them to move from Rany Bednore, where, by all accounts, I judge that they have been halted for about two months.[55]

Wellesley, like Cornwallis, understood the market principles of the Banjara's transport. He became anxious if they could not trade and, like Cornwallis, he sought to maintain their confidence through economic means.[56]

Yet on 27 May 1803 the future 'Iron' Duke of Wellington writes with an almost romantic despair about the Banjara. His frustration is that of a man deceived, once again, by a beautiful woman or perhaps by his own wayward son.

> The more I see of them, the more I am convinced that we have entirely mistaken the character of these people; and that unless they are permitted to plunder the country through which they pass, or to have profits such as the native armies are able to give them from plunder, they will not follow the troops to any distance from the place at which they usually reside. I have had the greatest difficulties with them, and they have deceived me, and broken their engagements upon every occasion. Colonel Stevenson who has another set, has been obliged to punish, and even to put some to death, for plunder in the Peshwah's country.[57]

OPPOSITE
Detail of cotton-thread embroidery on indigo and madder-dyed cotton, c. 1900. Maiwa collection.

OVERLEAF
Nurauva Rathod wearing her daily attire. She is standing next to her husband Umalaji Rathod. Commentators have often remarked on the difference between the ordinary clothing of the men and the elaborate dress of the women. Photographed outside their home, Gajendragad, Karnataka, 2013.

Cowrie pendant, a common addition to the waist strings of traditional Banjara skirts (such pendants are visible in the photo opposite).

The death penalty for plunder was not unusual. At the fall of Seringapatam, Wellesley had several of his own men flogged and four hanged to stop looting and restore order.[58] Wellesley writes again on 8 June 1803:

> I see very clearly that we have been too indulgent to the brinjarries. It may be said that the harsh treatment which Purneah [The Diwan of Mysore] always recommended would have driven many out of the Mysore country; but on the other hand, I have to acknowledge that the mild treatment which they have uniformly experienced has not brought them forward for the public service in the moment of need. They have deceived me in every instance they have broken every engagement they have made; and I think it not unlikely that I shall be in some distress, unless I can bring forward some of the brinjarries of this country.[59]

From this point on, Wellesley will try to depend less on the Banjara and work more with 'hired bullocks'. The British romance with the Banjara was coming to a close, just as, more generally, the romance of Englishmen who desired to integrate, marry into, and participate in India's native culture was coming to an end. The romance was replaced by the attitudes of men like Arthur Wellesley's elder brother, Richard Colley Wellesley, who arrived as India's governor-general in 1798. The elder Wellesley 'came to the governor-generalship not as a middle-class merchant, but as a New Mughal. He set a tone of aristocratic arrogance and high social style that was to become the model for generations of British proconsuls and servants of humbler rank.'[60]

MOST FEROCIOUS RUFFIANS

The British consolidation of control in India was the antithesis of the unending contest for power that marked the pre-colonial period. When a ruler died in the Mughal era, a series of destructive wars of succession could be expected until one dominant contender triumphed. If that ruler proved capable but short lived, as was the case with five-year rule of Aurangzeb's successor Shah Alam (r. 1707–12), the carnage (the equivalent of a full-scale civil war) would be repeated immediately. Dynastic rule was only as good (or bad) as the present monarch. 'Disputed successions, imbecilic contenders, and short reigns resulted in a rapid depletion of imperial resources, leading to administrative chaos and regional succession.'[61] One of the primary differences of rule under the British Raj was that those wielding power placed their personal ambition beneath that of the collective colonial machine.

There has never been a good time to be a peasant. The British Raj worked just as hard to extract revenues from the agrarian classes as did any other overlords. Nevertheless, in order to ensure that most of the surplus production made its way into British coffers, a new and systematic project of regulating and policing the countryside was implemented. For some this was an unforeseen benefit: 'Maratha brahmins would soon be able to tell their families in awed delight that a man could "carry gold at the top of his walking stick from Poona to Delhi without being molested by robbers."'[62] But for the Banjara, a group that would see its way of life move further and further outside the diminishing circle of colonial tolerance, it would prove disastrous.

From the great Mughals down to the smallest tribal chief, the unwritten law of ownership was that you owned only as much as you could defend. While the British clearly understood this principle during conquest or when constructing their fortified ports in civil government they hoped to govern through quite a different set of principles. As vast parts of the Indian map were coloured pink, systems of land ownership and revenue were overhauled: first in Bengal and later in southern India. Each of these systems would entrench a set of legal principles and rights based on private land ownership. Groups such as the Banjara, who were peripatetic, naturally fell afoul of these laws. Like aboriginal groups in Australia, Canada and the United States who found themselves marginalized by expanding colonial empires, the Banjara and their way of life was slowly being legislated out of existence.

The process began through increased regulation on Banjara cargo. Charges, taxes and duties would be payable at checkpoints and boarder crossings. This system was next extended to the oxen. In alignment with property rights, restrictions were placed on 'cattle trespass'. Finally, and most notoriously, restrictions were to be placed on the Banjara themselves. In 1871, the Criminal Tribes Act was passed. The act required all individual members of such tribes to register with the police.[63] The Banjara were treated as if the entire tribe had committed a crime and were now under surveillance and probation.

This photograph of young Banjara women was reproduced from a halftone in the 1928 edition of *The Mysore Tribes and Castes*, a publication that included Banjara living in the Shimoga Hills area. The young women are probably unmarried as they are not wearing bangles above the elbow or embroidered *kachali*.

Carrying water near Badami, Karnataka. Women's daily dress includes upper-arm bracelets and anklets made of rows of tiny lead balls, each containing a metal seed that makes them tinkle, a *kachali*, replete with mirrors, metal buttons, appliqué and embroidery, and a *phetiya* with a wide heavily embroidered band. In addition, this woman carries a waist bag covered in beadwork.

The sea-change in attitude towards the Banjara can be sensed from the report of Scottish physician Francis Buchanan, who travelled through Mysore in 1800, the year after Mysore fell to the British. Buchanan, whose journey was commissioned by elder (Marquis) Wellesley, was an adept scientist and a gifted botanist. He would go on to catalogue over 100 new species of fish in the river Ganges. Throughout his survey of Mysore, however, he repeatedly characterizes the Banjara using almost exactly the same phrase each time. The villagers 'having been plundered by the Brinjáries, or Lumbádies...the bulk of the inhabitants perished from hunger.'[64] It is not just the deficit of literary style that makes Buchanan's text suspect, his description is the first that appears to be openly prejudiced against the Banjara. It is also possible that he never personally met any Banjara and instead he relied on hearsay:

The chief plunderers were the rabble belonging to the Nizam, and the Brinjaries, who are most ferocious ruffians, that not only plunder, but wantonly murder, every defenseless person that comes their way. My interpreter, who was in the party coming up with Colonel Read, confirms the truth of what the natives say. No exertions of our officers could prevent the Brinjaries from plundering, not only the enemy, but the villages belonging to the Company that were in the neighbourhood of their route. Colonel Read's humanity and justice are too well known in the eastern parts of Mysore, for a single person there to imagine that every possible exertion for their safety was not employed.[65]

No less sensational was the account compiled by the Abbé Jean-Antoine Dubois, a French Catholic missionary who was in Mysore at roughly the same time as Buchanan. Dubois's text makes a zealous attempt to paint the Banjara as savages:

> But of all the nomadic castes which wander about the country, the best known and most detested is the Lambadis or Sukalers, or Brinjaris.... Of all the castes of the Hindus this particular one is acknowledged to be the most brutal. The natural proclivities of its members for evil are clearly indicated by their ill-favoured, wild appearance and their coarse, hard-featured countenances, these characteristics being as noticeable in the women as in the men. In all parts of India they are under the special supervision of the police, because there is only too much reason for mistrusting them.[66]

Such Catholic sentiment would not be complete without some sexual tension – and this is duly added:

> Their women are, for the most part, very ugly and revoltingly dirty. Amongst other glaring vices they are supposed to be much addicted to incontinency; and they are reputed to sometimes band themselves together in search of men whom they compel by force to satisfy their lewd desires.[67]

No other account, including the multitude written when the tribe is criminalized, confirms Dubois's claims. Moreover, there is evidence that the Dubois manuscript was not even written by Dubois. Instead, it was 'in large part based on an obscure manuscript written by Père Coeurdoux in the 1760s'.[68]

The acute need of the expanding British Raj to gather insider knowledge of India (supposedly of the kind supplied by Dubois) can be judged by the fact that Lord William Bentinck, then governor of Madras, purchased the manuscript for 8,000 rupees in 1807.[69] The purchase was reported by Bentinck to the Board of Directors of the East India Company as 'of great public importance'. The importance was driven by the fact that as British presence grew, casual interactions between the English and natives decreased. The new English attitude was to remain aloof, ever hopeful that despite the climate, English life and English customs might be re-created in India. British forces were large enough to require completely separate cantonments and in their isolated Presidency offices the 'New Mughals' who made the key decisions would have little chance or need to mingle. Bentinck was Governor-General of India from 1828 until 1835. In his comments on the need for the Dubois manuscript he states:

Centre square from a *garna* (a cloth used to cover water pots). The bands that would surround it have been removed and made into other items, Karnataka, *c.* 1970. Maiwa collection.

We do not, we cannot, associate with the natives. We cannot see them in their houses and with their families. We are necessarily very much confined to our houses by the heat; all our wants and business which would create a greater intercourse with the natives is done for us and we are, in fact strangers in the land.[70]

It may seem shocking today that a group 'very much confined to our houses' could gain control over the entire subcontinent, but Bentinck's comments echoed the sentiments of Scottish historian, James Mill, who claimed: 'A man who is duly qualified may obtain more knowledge of India, in one year, in his closet in England, than he could obtain during the course of the longest life, by the use of his eyes and ears in India.'[71] Mill might have been trying to justify his authorship of the three-volume *The History of British India* in the face of the obvious objection that he knew no Indian languages; nor had he, in fact, ever visited the place.

Milder (and perhaps more accurate) accounts of the Banjara would not receive nearly the wealth of official notice as the works of Buchanan, Dubois and Mill did.

BHANGI'S BULLOCKS

Noticeably absent from much Banjara history is the voice of the Banjara themselves. Apart from Moor, Wilks and Briggs few chroniclers of the colonial period mention who they have interviewed. In part, this is simply due to the times, in part it is due to the desire to create an omniscient and authoritative text and in part it is the result of the fact that the Banjara maintained an oral culture.

One story in particular seems to have been told and retold in different guises with different details. It is the story of the Banjara chief, Bhangi Naik, the man from the Rathod clan who commanded the greatest horde of Bullocks ever assembled.

No little textural forensics is necessary to determine the original source or the lineage of the story. The most widespread version (at first) also appears to be the most credible. It was written by Mr N. F. Cumberlege, Superintendent of Police in Wún District (now Yavatmal), in 1869.[72]

Cumberlege writes that around 1630, during the reign of Shah Jahan (r. 1628–58) two brothers Bhangi and Jhangi Naik had with them 180,000 bullocks, they accompanied 'A'saf Ján, sometimes called A'saf Khan, the Vazir of Sháh Jehán'. A bullock-train comprising tens of thousands of beasts, however, is an unwieldy force of its own. To ensure that the caravans kept up with the army,

A'saf Ján...was induced to give an order to Bhangi and Jhangi Náiks, as they put forward excuses regarding the difficulty obtaining grass and water for their cattle. This order was engraved on copper and in gold letters, as follows : –

Ranjan ka páni,
Chapar ka ghás,
Din ka tín khún maaf.
Aur juhán A'saf Ján ke ghore,
Wahán Bhangi Jhangi ke báil

The meaning of the inscription seems to be: If you can find no water elsewhere, you may even take it from the pots of my followers; grass you may take from the roof of their huts; and if you commit three murders a day I will even pardon this, provided that where I find my cavalry I can always find Bhangi Jhangi's bullocks.[73]

This legendary copper plate marks the height of Banjara power: they are literally able to get away with murder. Additional details of the tale, however, including a conflict that takes place directly after the patent is awarded, seem to be set during the time of the first Nizam of Hyderabad. This would place the action at least a century later. If the awarding of the copper plate is taken in isolation, the inconsistency is not apparent. Edward Balfour (who we will meet later) solved this riddle by moving the date ahead to 1730. By assuming 'Asof Jah' to be the first Nizam of Hyderabad he made a more consistent story.[74]

In 1814, at the invitation of the Literary Society of Bombay, John Briggs collected his notes from extensive interviews with the Banjara near Hyderabad and presented a comprehensive essay on Banjara history and customs. In his essay Briggs repeats a more colourful version of what might be called 'the tale of Bhangi's Bullocks'. In his telling, the chief of the Rathore clan is named Sarung and is nicknamed Bhungy after his propensity to take bhung (an intoxicating mixture of cannabis, milk and ghee). Sarung Bhungy at the command of 180,000 head of oxen is given the patent to bring supplies to the imperial army during Aurangzeb's campaigns against Golconda and Bijapur in the 1680s. At the same time Bhungy is given a standard and granted three 'privileges'

1. To take the thatch from off all houses when grain is scarce.
2. To appropriate to their own use all water which may be found in pots ready drawn for the use of the family.
3. Indiscriminate plunder in the enemy's country.[75]

Such privileges were not, however, extended to Bhungy's rival, Bhugwan Burteeah. The rivalry became acrimonious. Clan violence followed with attacks and retribution flowing between the Rathore and Burteeah groups. The last conflict between the two clans took place at Ramagoorum on the banks of the Crishna (Krishna) river – it was a particularly bloody meeting and the Burteeahs left victorious with the standard and the patent. Briggs writes that both are reported to be still in the possession of the Burteeah Naik who resides in the city of Hyderabad.[76]

James Tod, writing of his encounter with a group in Rasjasthan during the 1820s, reports that he was 'taken prisoner' by them:

I was highly gratified with the reception I received from the community, which collectively advanced to me at some distance from the town. The procession was headed by the village-band and all the fair Chārunis, who, as they approached, gracefully waved their scarfs over me, until I was fairly made captive by the muses of Murlāh![77]

The act was a reenactment of an hereditary right that the Banjara claimed: to take any passing king prisoner and ransom him for a feast.

It was not until the afternoon, when the naiques again came to see me at my camp, that I learned the full value of my escape from the silken bonds of the fair Charunis. This community had enjoyed for five hundred years the privilege of making prisoner any Rana [king] of Méwar who may pass through Murlah, and keeping him in bondage until he gives them a gote, or entertainment; and their chains are neither galling, nor the period of captivity, being thus in the hands of the captivated, very long. The patriarch told me that I was in jeopardy, as the Rana's representative; but not knowing how I might have relished the joke, had it been carried to its conclusion, they let me escape, though they lost a feast by it.[78]

Upon hearing the detail of the tradition, Tod tells them that he is 'too much delighted with old customs' not to participate; and so, while he remains with the naiks talking, he sends money to the women for a feast.

Almost 60 years later another traveller, the Irish geologist and orthinologist Valentine Ball, was working his way along the Mahanadi river in what is now Odisha, happily shooting rare birds in the spirit of John James Audubon. Ball's encounter is a shadow of Tod's experience.

To-day when passing through the village of Labanatand, a sort of standing camp or depôt of the Labanos or Brinjaras, I was at once struck by the peculiar costumes and brilliant clothing of these Indian gipsies. They immediately recalled to my memory the appearance of the Zingari of the lower Danube and Wallachia. In about two minutes I was surrounded by all the women of the place, who commenced to chant and escort me across the fields. This attention, however, I declined, as I was at work and did not care for their company, and they retired, somewhat crestfallen at my repelling them. Afterwards, however, in the evening two parties about thirty strong each, came to the camp and sang for an hour or so in the peculiarly melancholy minor key which characterizes all the music of these people which I have heard.[79]

Ball relates in a footnote that a Hungarian nobleman, travelling in India in 1874, was able to 'converse with the Brinjaras of Central India, in consequence of his knowledge of the Zingari language'. It is a piece in the long-standing puzzle of the origin of the European Roma – a linguistic lead connecting the Roma and their ancestors to the Banjara.

The following day, while continuing his journey, Ball encountered a second group who also came out to meet him. A woman went so far as to seize the bridle of his horse:

To-day I passed through another Brinjara hamlet, from whence the women and girls all hurried out in pursuit, and a brazen-faced powerful-looking lass seized the bridle of my horse as he was being led by the sayce in the rear. The sayce and chuprasi were both Mahomedans, and the forward conduct of these females perplexed them not a little, and the former was fast losing his temper at being thus assaulted by a woman; nolens volens [willing or unwilling] they wished to persuade me to stop to listen to their singing again, but the previous day's performance had been quite sufficient for me.[80]

Song and dance continue to be the key vessels transporting traditional Banjara culture from one generation to the next.

ABOVE
A group of women form a circle in preparation for a dance. Wearing red headscarves covered in mirrors and embroidery, such groups have impressed observers for centuries. The most notable songs are the *devolo*, sung to celebrate a bride's journey from her parents' home to her new family. The melancholy nature of these songs suggests they mark the end of childhood and the beginning of an adult life filled with hard work and struggle, Sandur, Karnataka, 2005.

OPPOSITE
Dancing at the UNESCO Embroidery Conference, Hyderabad, 2001.

Empire of the Caravan | 59

POETS BY BIRTH

At the close of the Third Anglo-Maratha War, the British once again found themselves in control of large sections of new territory; as before they required a survey of the established cultures of their new acquisitions to assess revenue and collection practices. John Malcolm, the general who led the charge at the Battle of Mahidpur against the Peshwa's army, was also a historian and literary man. He was the obvious choice to furnish the survey.

In January 1818, Malcolm was put in charge of what was then called the Central Provinces and he spent the next four years collecting information – including oral histories – for his reports.[81] His very readable two-volume work *A Memoir of Central India* communicates an astonishing amount of detail concerning the new territories. He remarks, for example, that in some areas, the transit tax on pack-bullocks actually went down, as the collectors became aware that the drivers could use alternative routes, and that as a means of encouraging more benign collecting, the number of bullocks was rounded down to the lowest hundred. This gentle treatment may have just offset another small tax that no one was exempt from, called 'Koower Sookree': money for the Prince's breakfast.[82]

Malcolm also describes an advanced system of insurance and duty brokerage. This system, far from being disrupted by political instability, appears to be motivated by it. Malcolm claims that it was a clear notion of self-interest combined with 'a respect for certain classes and a veneration for established usages' that existed in the mind of even the most unjust princes of India, which permitted trade and business to continue amid anarchy.

Without military backing, the Banjara were liable for duties and taxes on their cargo. Although they received favourable rate compared to other classes and no insurance was needed for their bulky cargo, they could still be indentured to predatory financiers.

> The monied men, who engage in this line, have as commanding an influence over Brinjarries and the owners of cattle, as those Soucars who engage in revenue concerns have over the cultivators. They make the Brinjarries advances at high interest, and then monopolize the power of employing them; rendering by this process the recovery of their money secure and the carriers dependent.[83]

Malcolm observes human trafficking in which the Banjara (along with other groups) are implicated. These were sometimes female children sold by desperate families, however, abductions also occurred. Interestingly, the children were often sold as displaced high-caste Brahmins or Rajputs. 'The children are taught to make pretensions to high birth; and daily instances occur of whole families [who have purchased children] losing caste in consequence of these being too hastily credited.' Malcolm appears not only to have observed this human trafficking but also to have intervened in the recovery of some of the children.[84] Of the Banjara, Malcolm has written:

> They live in tents, and can hardly be termed inhabitants of any particular province, as every place where they pitch is their home, and that of their families.... Their number in any one province rises or falls like an article in trade, according to demand.

He calls them an industrious race, 'who live in a society of their own, and preserve, both in dress and usages, a marked separation and independence.' On land – using pack-bullocks instead of ships – the Banjara are almost identical to the British traders.

> They often engage in great speculations on their own account, and are deemed honest in their dealings.... They trust much to the bankers and merchants with whom they are concerned, and few keep accounts; but habit has made them very acute, and their memory is, from continual exercise, extremely retentive of the minutest particulars of their extended transactions.[85]

A Banjara Man and his Two Wives in their Gorgeous Costumes reproduced from *The Mysore Tribes and Castes.* Traditional Banjara culture permitted a widow to remarry. If a man died, it was acceptable for his younger brother to take the widow as a second wife. This tradition worked to keep the larger family intact and ensure that the children remained in the community. The man is holding a hookah (the mouthpiece has been detached from the bowl) and wearing an embroidered shoulder bag.

Working at the same time as Malcolm but further north and with much less regard for impartiality, James Tod was collecting information for his own romantic history of Rajasthan. Officially, Tod was charged with negotiating the treaties that brought the Rajput chieftains under British suzerainty, but he was more than a little enchanted with the martial qualities of the Rajputs. In them he saw a people who retained a sense of chivalric honour. In the territory about to become Rajasthan he saw a chessboard on which the feuds and rivalries of lords and vassals could be played out on a grand scale, giving ample subject matter to the native bards and poets. In short, he saw the Rajputs as feudal Europeans and it would be under this assumption that he would compile his massive opus. Tod observed the Banjara and thought that the entire tribe were once Bhats (bards) who had taken up carriage:

> Murlāh is an excellent township inhabited by a community of Chārans of the tribe Cucholia (Kacheli), who are Bunjārris (carriers) by profession, though poets by birth. The alliance is a curious one, and would appear incongruous were not gain the object generally in both cases. It was the sanctity of their office which converted our bardais (bards) into bunjārris, for their persons being sacred, the immunity extended likewise to their goods and saved them from all imposts; so that in process of time they became the free-traders of Rājputāna.[86]

Malcolm claims that the Banjara are not molested out of princely self-interest, while Tod maintains it was their ties to the sacred role of the bard that privileged them. No doubt it was a portion of each in addition to their spirited nature and well-established place in society:

> The tānda or caravan, consisting of four thousand bullocks, has been kept up amidst all the evils which have beset this land through Mughal and Marātha tyranny. The utility of these caravans as general carriers to conflicting armies and as regular tax-paying subjects has proved their safeguard, and they were too strong to be pillaged by any petty marauder, as any one who has seen a Banjāri encampment will be convinced. They encamp in a square, and their grain-bags piled over each other breast-high, with interstices left for their matchlocks, make no contemptible fortification.[87]

Tod mentions another instance of military commanders attempting to ingratiate themselves with the merchants and the gift of another patent:

> Even the ruthless Tūrk, Jamshīd Khān, set up a protecting tablet in favour of the Chārans of Murlāh, recording their exemption from dīnd contributions, and that there should be no increase in duties, with threats to all who should injure the community. As usual, the sun and moon are appealed to as witnesses of good faith, and sculptured on the stone. Even the forest Bhīl and mountain Mair have set up their signs of immunity and protection to the chosen of Hinglāz (tutelary deity); and the figures of a cow and its kairi (calf) carved in rude relief speak the agreement that they should not be slain or stolen within the limits of Murlāh.[88]

But it was their independent spirit and appearance that moved him most.

A man's bag similar to the one being worn in the photograph opposite. Bags like these have pockets inside each of the four sides and are usually a marriage gift. A man may keep a variety of items in his bag, including areca nuts (also known as betel or *supari*), tobacco and money. Maiwa collection, *c.* 1920.

It was a novel and interesting scene: the manly persons of the Chārans, clad in the flowing white robe, with the high loose-folded turban inclined on one side, from which the māla or chaplet was gracefully suspended; and the naiques or leaders, with their massive necklaces of gold, with the image of the pitriswar (manes) depending therefrom, gave the whole an air of opulence and dignity. The females were uniformly attired in a skirt of dark-brown camlet, having a bodice of light-coloured stuff, with gold ornaments worked into their fine black hair; and all had the favourite chooris or rings of háti-dânt (elephant's tooth), covering the arm from the wrist to the elbow, and even above it.[89]

Following in the footsteps of Tod's glowing prose was the portrait furnished by Scottish physician Edward Balfour. In 1843, Balfour penned the following contribution to Jameson's *The Edinburgh New Philosophical Journal*,

Their features are dark and bronzed. The men have tall and muscular frames. Their dress, differing much from the nations and communities around them, attracts attention to the females of the tribe, on whom nature has bestowed the most faultless forms; tall and exquisitely moulded, these dark children of the desert move with a grace unwitnessed among a civilized people, their loose and peculiarly formed garments assisting to set off their shape.[90]

After describing the people, Balfour goes on to note their 'loose and peculiarly formed garments':

A boddice (called Kanterie) fitting neatly into the form in front, reaches from the neck to the hip, conceals the bosom, but is left open behind; this with a gown (petia) fastened by a noose beneath the waist, and falling in loose folds to the feet, and scarf (cadhi) thrown carelessly over the shoulder, completes their dress, which is made of cloth dyed with bright and varied colours. From their hair, and the tapes that bind their dress, are suspended long strings of courie shells, massive rings of silver clasp the ankles, and the arms, from the wrist to the shoulder, are loaded with broad rings of ivory, cut from the elephants' tusks, and dyed with varied dyes.[91]

Balfour was a British officer, a medical man, and an environmentalist who saw the deforestation of India as a public health problem. He founded the Government Museum at Madras in 1850 and was the first officer in charge. By 1879 the museum was admitting 180,000 people each year (attracted, no doubt, by his policy of free admission). Women visitors were encouraged on special days. He was also a cyclopaedist who edited the first three editions of the *Cyclopaedia of India*. The third edition explicitly mentions the fine nature of Banjara embroidery.

They are capital needle-women, making their own jackets and petticoats, and frequently embroider these tastefully. The material used by the women of some branches of this tribe is manufactured from the fibre of a species of nettle, which is woven into cloth for themselves, and these are tastefully dyed...to suit their peculiar taste in this respect, frequently over-gaudy.[92]

Balfour was an orientalist of seemingly limitless industry. In addition to the museum he started a public library in Madras. He made good use of his fluency in

ABOVE
A Woman of the Tribe of Indian Gipsies known as Lumbadi from the 1914 edition of *Southern India*. Painted by Lady Lawley and described by F. E. Benny, the book retells much of what is found in John Briggs's account.

OPPOSITE
Chavlibai is an elder of Malavagoppa tanda, a Banjara settlement located just outside the city limits of Shimoga, Karnataka. Chavlibai is wearing her daily outfit, which includes all her gold jewelry, Malavagoppa, Karnataka, 2014.

OVERLEAF
A group of Banjara women have gathered together in their festive dress to be photographed, near Badami, Karnataka, 2013.

Hindi and Persian to translate not only poetic and historic works into English, but also Dr T. Conquest's *Outlines of Midwifery* into Hindi. Balfour's views were openly anti-colonialist, sentiments he seems to have shared with his uncle, Joseph Hume, and cousin Allan Octavian Hume (one of the founders of the Indian National Congress). Balfour wrote beautifully about the Banjara:

> They recognize no Civil Authority, keep aloof from settled races, interfere with no one, and allow of no interference among them in the matter of their laws or customs, etc. As carriers, distance and climate have no difficulties for them. They undertake extensive engagements exporting merchandise, chiefly, grain, cotton, cloths, oil-seeds, etc., and carry them out with the utmost good faith. They never play false once when the work is undertaken by them; no instance has been known of goods entrusted to their care having been robbed. They are looked upon by other classes of natives with superstitous dread, so that they can traverse the wildest and most jungly tracts with impunity and perfect security.[93]

It seems a description that Banjara would be proud to read today.

ETHNOGRAPHIC CRIMINALS

If the British saw themselves as Bentinck claimed, as 'strangers in the land' that they ruled, some mechanism would need to be devised to inform the legions of administrators, magistrates, collectors, police and petty officials about the unusual customs of the bewildering variety of peoples in the country they were expected to govern. At this time, the British vested considerable authority in the printed word. They were a 'People of the Book' in the sense that the Koran intended, but also, and perhaps more importantly, in the sense that 'texts' (religious, legislative, or encyclopedic) were considered the real site of authority. Such a bibliocentric culture was prejudiced to believe that oral histories were necessarily evanescent and ephemeral; they were not to be trusted and hardly believed. In a statement that became infamous, Thomas Macaulay clearly annunciated the British mistrust of oral knowledge and their dismissive regard for Indian texts. In his 1835 *Minute on Education* he stated:

> It is, I believe, no exaggeration to say, that all the historical information which has been collected from all the books written in the Sanskrit language is less valuable than what may be found in the most paltry abridgments used at preparatory schools in England.[94]

Clearly early nineteenth-century officials were in the wilderness – stationed in outposts without even a telegraph (the first lines went up in 1851). Communication, in an official sense, was almost exclusively written, which resulted in an impressive archive of dispatches, letters and missives. But these were to be dwarfed by the groaning shelves of printed volumes about to be produced. Gazetteers, with maps, descriptions of terrain, listings of villages and settlements; manuals for districts, containing histories and overviews of agriculture and manufacturing; census reports giving statistics about income, religion, revenue, trade and education;

Pulia embroidered with tiny mirrors and cowries, Mysore, Karnataka, *c.* 1910. Maiwa collection.

and through all of these books ran a substantial ethnographic component that attempted to fix through the printed word complete descriptions of the peoples of India: their ethnogenesis, dress, manners, habits, skills, ceremonies for marriage and death, language, religion, location, caste and tribe.

The ethnographic project was undertaken on a scale that was equal to the breadth and range of India itself. It was an ever expanding attempt to make a map that was the same scale as the territory – with the key exception that this ethnographic map was made of words – for the volumes were at best sparsely illustrated.

Through this encyclopedic project the character of the Banjara was to be fixed and understood. They would be defined and categorized. This was not an academic or abstract endeavour, for in a very real sense to write the description of who a people were was already to have gained control and mastery over them.

It is impossible to form an understanding of the Banjara today without also understanding their relationship to the British Raj. In many ways it was the collision of two merchant empires. On the one hand were the medieval Banjara, who were organized along clan and family lines, who enjoyed an oral culture, who speculated on their own account in long-distance trade on a grand scale and who had little heed for concepts (or indeed the claims) of private property rights. On the other hand were the modern British who were organized as a chartered company and later a colonial empire, who encouraged a paper-based culture with a fine bureaucratic nuance – where the threshold of participation was set by basic literacy – and who deployed a judicial and revenue system that enshrined the idea of private property. From the British perspective the very existence of the Banjara was a dangerous criticism of their ideology. Moreover, because the British had actually worked with the Banjara and depended on them, it was not possible to view the itinerant merchants as an isolated or primitive tribe who only refused the gifts of civilization through ignorance. The Banjara knew the British and the British knew the Banjara.

The loss of Banjara privilege follows a timeline that is directly tied to the modernization of India. With the end of the Maratha Wars in 1818, the British would consolidate the process of dismantling the 'ancien régime' economies and re-visioning them under capitalist, utilitarian and mercantile principles. The result was a swift process of 'peasantization' wherein:

> Displaced soldiers, courtiers, priests and artisans found their way onto the
> land, which was fast becoming the only available base of subsistence. They
> were joined, too, by increasing numbers of pastoralists and forest peoples.
> Road building programmes, undertaken as much for military as for economic
> reasons, undermined the Banjara economy, while policies of rapid forest clearance
> and the forced settlement of mobile peoples reduced the peripatetic elements
> in the economy.[95]

In the north the Banjara were also seen as an impediment to settling forest and mountain tracts. Modern histories blame the introduction of railways for destroying the Banjara way of life. In fact, many of the conditions that made long-distance ox caravans possible had been eliminated before the first rolling stock hit the rails.

ABOVE
Pulia worked in counted brick stitch, Khandesh, *c.* 1940. Maiwa collection.

OVERLEAF LEFT
Four *pulia* showing vibrant colour schemes adopted once synthetic dyed threads came into local markets, Karnataka, *c.* 1980. Maiwa collection.

OVERLEAF RIGHT
Four *pulia* showing the counted cross-stitch work of Khandesh. The two lower *pulia* feature cross stitch bordered by appliqué work, *c.* 1920. Maiwa collection.

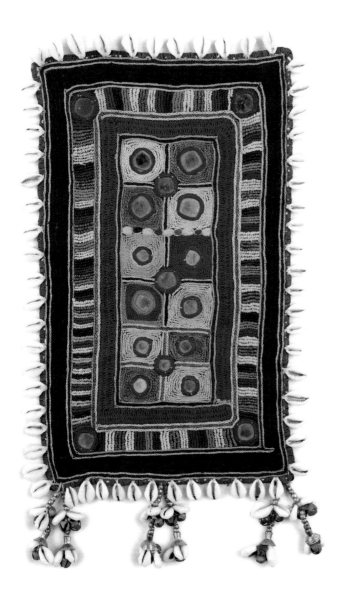
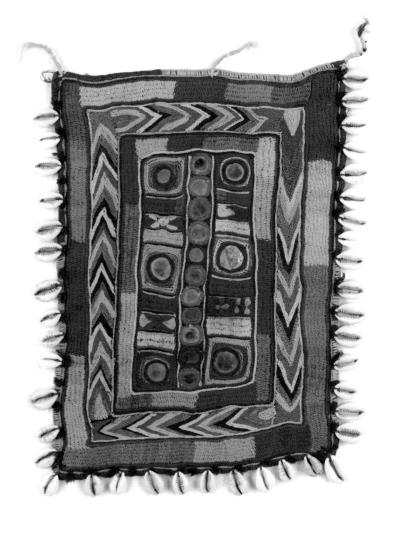

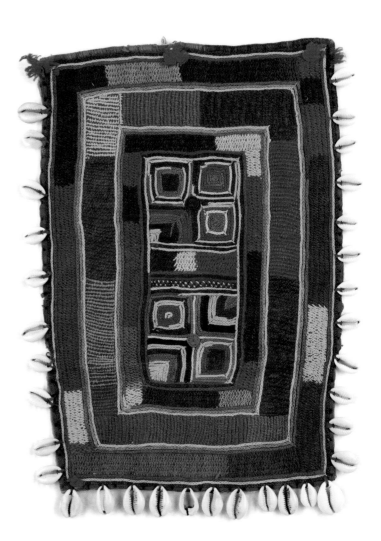

In British territories the Banjara role was restricted by three developments: first they were more closely subordinated to merchant groups and to the military commissariat department; secondly, their pasture land was gradually restricted by advancing agriculture; and finally a series of cattle epidemics in Malwa and Rajasthan in the 1820s and 1830s broke up some of the largest bands with remarkable speed.[96]

Salt, for example, was the principle cargo of the Banjara sub-group known as the Lambada, who transported it inland to the central provinces in exchange for cotton, which they brought back to the coastal textile industry. The scale and complexity of the trade was staggering. In a single 'salt season' between '70,000 and 120,000 bullocks were expected to visit each of eight major salt-trading centres along the south-east coast.'[97] Salt had been taxed in Mughal times, however, the British sought not only to tax it, but also to monopolize the trade. Later, salt would form the iconic basis of Mahatma Gandhi's gesture of resistance when on 6 April 1930 he picked up a handful of salt and proclaimed the end of the British Empire in India. For the Banjara, an indication of how seriously the British took customs duties is given by the construction of the Inland Customs Line, or as it has been characterized by Roy Moxham, The Great Hedge of India:

> A customs line was established, which stretched across the whole of India, which in 1869 extended from the Indus to the Mahanadi in Madras, a distance of 2,300 miles; and it was guarded by nearly 12,000 men and petty officers.... It consisted principally of an immense impenetrable hedge of thorny trees and bushes, supplemented by stone wall and ditches, across which no human being or beast of burden or vehicle could pass without being subject to detention or search.[98]

The mechanisms through which Banjara trade was eroded in the south are mapped in considerable detail in Bhangya Bhukya's book *Subjugated Nomads: The Lambadas under the Rule of the Nizams*. There he describes how economic policies slowly squeezed out the Banjara merchants and made long-distance carriage impractical.[99]

At the same time as the cargo was regulated, steps were taken to dismantle the considerable 'cattle wealth' that the Banjara still held. During military campaigns the Banjara enjoyed the rights of trespass. In pre-colonial peacetime, the relationship between the settled peasants and the Banjara was negotiated, with the oxen manuring the fields they passed through and the Banjara compensating for damage through the supply of milk, ghee, barter of animal husbandry skills and sometimes payment for damage in oxen. The new colonial paradigm, however, was based on the privilege of private property: 'cattle trespass' was first regulated in 1816 in the Madras Presidency. Owners of itinerant cattle could be fined or the animals could be seized and auctioned.[100]

For many of the itinerant merchants, switching to agriculture was the obvious solution. It involved a radical cultural shift, however, as their traditions and skills were neither agrarian nor sedentary. Moreover, for some Banjara clans their Rajput lineage prohibited serfdom:

OPPOSITE
Pulia made of indigo-dyed wool with cotton-thread embroidery, Shimoga Hills, *c.* 1940. Maiwa collection.

Empire of the Caravan | 73

[The Banjara's] occupations, strictly speaking, ought to be confined to a military life; and in this tribe also is the lineal succession of royalty preserved. The Rujpoot may cultivate with his own hands his own land; but he must not work as a villain for another, he can only serve as a soldier; but custom permits him to perform many things for himself that it would be disgraceful for him to do as the menial of another.[101]

Soon, however, they would have little choice.

On 16 April 1853 at 3.35 pm a train with 14 railway carriages and 400 guests left Bombay's Bori Bunder platform with a 21-gun salute.[102] It was India's first passenger train and its departure marked the beginning of India's love affair with the railways. The railways were also the most effective way to get British finished goods into India and get a variety of raw materials including cotton and timber from the forest areas out. The network would expand considerably under Viceroy Richard Bourke, whose focus on railroads and canals in the 1870s was satirized as 'Trains and Drains' administration. The railways brought the caravan trade to a decisive end. The vast herds of pack-bullocks that sometimes stretched up to 20 miles in length and took days to pass would never be seen again.

Qualities that were necessary to survive as successful long-distance carriers (fierce independence and a martial nature) made the Banjara tenacious settlers who flourished in more isolated areas. In the first settlement report of the 'Goojerat District' in 1861 Captain Hector MacKenzie observed that the Banjara capitalized on instability:

Latterly they have taken to agriculture, but as an additional means of livelihood not as a substitute for trade. As a section of the community they deserve every consideration and encouragement. They are generally fine substantially built people. They also posses much spirit. In anarchical times when the freaks or feuds of petty Governors would drive the Jats or Gujars to seek a temporary abiding place away from their ancestral village, the Labanas [Banjara] would stand their ground and perhaps improve the opportunity by extending their grasp over the best lands in the village.[103]

In the region north of Delhi groups of Muslim Banjara are to be found. By the time the British conducted the 1881 census 30 per cent of the Banjara population in the North-West Provinces claimed Sikh affiliation.[104] The census records also identify several large Banjara peasant communities in the central India districts. In 1880 they were still an 'unsettled tribe' in Khandesh (a region in the Bombay Presidency). The *Gazetteer* gives a frank assessment:

Careful in matters of accounts, of simple habits and of a saving disposition, they promise to become a wealthy class of cultivators, and when they lose their strange beliefs about witchcraft and death they will prove a tractable and useful tenantry.[105]

Groups that did not turn to agriculture found their ability to move increasingly restricted. With neither land nor a caravan trade they gradually retreated into the forested regions where they maintained cattle and harvested firewood.

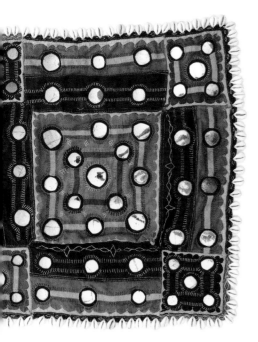

ABOVE
A *garna* embroidered with mirrors, appliqué and cowries. These cloths are used to cover water pots, either while being carried or during ceremonies, 58 cm square, *c.* 1980. Maiwa collection.

OPPOSITE
Embroidered band for a woman's skirt. This piece is sparsely embroidered and framed with appliqué, *c.* 1970. Maiwa collection.

In southern India, however, moving into the forest regions placed them in conflict with other adivasi groups as well as with the conservation officers charged with protecting forest resources.

As intruders, these Banjara received little sympathy in times of drought, famine, or when epidemic disease struck their cattle. As one assistant conservator at Warangal stated:

> A large number of cattle died during the year for want of fodder and water but I do not see that it is a cause for regret as the people had kept immense numbers of utterly useless cattle and it was mostly these which died as, generally speaking, care was taken by owners to incur even extra expense to keep alive those cattle which were really worth having.[106]

It was under such conditions that many Banjara returned to plunder as a more lucrative way of living.

It must be remembered that in the pre-colonial military culture, the opportunity to plunder was used strategically; it motivated irregulars to harass enemy territory and it helped incite poorly paid troops to victory in battle. The Banjara, who were constantly in military service up to the first quarter of the nineteenth century, were familiar with this ethos. When combined with a militant view towards private ownership; 'Theft by them, as among the Spartans is not considered a crime'[107] and when exacerbated by the loss of the caravan trade, the fact that Banjara turned to plunder during hard times or as an attractive alternative to peasantization is unsurprising.

A robbery made by a gang of five or more was termed a 'dacoity'. A member of such a gang was a 'dacoit'. The fact that groups of Banjara engaged in dacoity is not disputed. To deal with this and a range of similar crimes, the British set up the Thuggee and Dacoity Department in 1830. Championed by Sir William Henry Sleeman, the sensational narratives of thuggee crimes (ritualized murders, committed after befriending unwary travellers) are horrific enough to make inaction unthinkable. Like the report of an atrocity that stirs a nation to war, reports of thuggee worked to mobilize public sentiment and increase police funding. Thuggee was characterized as both hereditary and an artifact of the caste system. It was both normal and deviant. Its presence was used to legitimate the criminalization of elements of Indian society who were 'unproductive' in an economic sense and a potential source of anti-government agitation. Not surprisingly, these included many itinerant groups caught by the peasantization process such as the Banjara.

The question of whether the natives could be trusted took on new importance after the Indian Rebellion of 1857. In an important sense, the rebellion can be seen as a failure of cultural knowledge. The spark that ignited growing discontent into open revolt was the introduction of new cartridges for the Enfield rifle: greased with pork fat and beef tallow, they required the soldier to bite the cartridge open. Thus they were offensive to both Muslims and Hindus. Even though the cartridges were quickly withdrawn, the episode seemed to confirm suspicions that the British were attempting to christianize Indians through forced loss of caste status.[108] The surprising preponderance of detail on the cultural habits of different groups that

appeared in the manuals and gazetteers produced by the colonial government after the rebellion was intended to redress this failure of cultural knowledge. But the rebellion had brought into brilliant relief a question of trust and so the ethnography also included an important consideration of criminality.

The Criminal Tribes Act was brought forward in 1871. Like earlier legislation promulgated in late medieval England that was designed to curb vagrancy it criminalized entire groups, not for actions, but by classification. To be a gypsy was to be *de facto* a criminal.[109] Membership in the group precluded innocence. In India the classification was aptly provided by the anthropological and ethnographic mapping of the imperium. On such a map, the Banjara found themselves classified as a predatory caste: habituated and addicted to crime.

The classification would stigmatize Banjara not only in the eyes of the police, but also in the eyes of other castes, their fellow Indians, and themselves. The criminalization induced what is now called 'historical trauma'. The term is most commonly used in an aboriginal context to describe such group experiences as the residential schools of North American first nations. It is a 'cumulative emotional and psychological wounding, across generations, caused by significant group traumatic experiences.'[110] Its results are well documented and include substance abuse, poverty, unemployment and alcoholism. It is not possible to remove the stigma simply by removing a group from the list. In a move typical of Indian bureaucracy, a group who were no longer a 'criminal tribe' became an 'ex-criminal tribe' or a 'denotified tribe'. These terms carry similar connotations to 'ex-con'. In some Indian states the Banjara are still petitioning for the more neutral status of 'scheduled caste'.

Under the Criminal Tribes Act local governments could apply to have a 'tribe, gang or class' declared 'criminal'. Members were then obliged to report for registration. It was an offence not to report. The group could be moved or relocated to 'reformation' settlements and individuals were required to report on a regular basis to the police. It was an offence for individuals to be outside the prescribed area and they needed to apply for permission and receive a pass if they wished to travel.[111] The act was expedient to remove indigenous peoples from resource-rich areas and to settle itinerants, nomads, or suspicious populations forcibly. The act also nicely shifted the cause of criminality away from socio-economic circumstance (which might be directly traceable to colonial economic policy) onto 'hereditary' caste or tribal traits that were deemed to be as inflexible as they were peculiar.

TRIBE, CASTE, RACE

In 1882, Major Edward James Gunthorpe of the Berar Police published his *Notes on the Criminal Tribes*.[112] It was originally published in the *Times of India* as a kind of Victorian 'true crime' report tailored for colonial readers. It was later published in book form, in the hopes that the public, especially those whose duty brings them into constant contact with the 'predatory classes', might find it useful. The longest section is on the Banjara, with a second section on the Mooltanee (Muslim Banjara). In what is surely an ironic condemnation, the Mooltanee are

A woman of Sigatiranakairi tanda, Karnataka, 2013. The *kachali* of this tanda are all stylistically identical, the only variation is the colour of the ground fabric. It is likely that a nearby tailor services the clothing needs of the tanda.

accused of stealing opium. The British (by contrast) forced opium on China through strength of arms, against Chinese law, and ratified the drug trade in the Treaty of Nanking.

> The Kaynjur Mooltanees are professional dacoits, highway robbers and cattle-lifters, but not burglars. They are addicted to robbing opium, and may rightly be termed 'opium dacoits'. This drug, or other merchandize, is more generally robbed while in transit along the principal roads, either whilst the convoy is on the move or encamped.[113]

In 1892, ten years later, Frederick S. Mullaly, a senior officer of the Madras Police, published a similar volume. It was hoped that it might be useful to his fellow police officers. Mullaly notes that 'the facts have, for the most part, been verified by personal association with the people themselves'. Mullaly's entry on the Banjara is much quoted in later publications and the content is a disconcerting blend of ethnography and criminology. In *Notes on the Criminal Classes of the Madras Presidency* Mullaly writes:

> The women are, as a rule, comely, and above the average height of women of the country. They are easily identified by their dress and the profusion of jewels they wear.

> Their costume is the 'lainga' or gown of Karwar cloth, red or green, with a quantity of embroidery. The chola or bodice, with embroidery in the front and on the shoulders, covers the bosom and is tied by variegated cords at the back, the ends of the cords being ornamented with cowries and beads; a covering cloth of Karwar cloth, with embroidery, is fastened in at the waist and hangs at the side with a quantity of tassels and strings of cowries....

> They are clever herdsmen and are frequently employed by villagers to tend their cattle, in this way, and from friendly liquor-vendors, much information is gained as to itinerant parties...[114]

One of the first photographs ever taken of the Banjara, it appears in volume 7 of *The People of India* (plate number 366). The photographer is Lieut. James Waterhouse, who also noted the ages of the sitters and the colours of the garments. The photograph was probably taken near Indore in 1862.[115] The text reads as follows:

BRINJARIES
The man wears a red and white turban, a white tunic and dhoty and a red scarf over his shoulders. He is sitting on his feet closed together, a posture peculiar to Brinjaries, leaning on his spear shaft, and his hookah stands by him; his sword is across his knees. He is five feet six inches in height and thirty years old. The woman is Rattan, five feet two inches in height, and fifty years old.... She wears a great many ornaments, a gold or gilt ring through the nose, massive silver ear ornaments, silver and gold chains and neck ornaments, silver bracelets and anklets, and the high comb peculiar to the Brinjari women.... It is strange that no good pictures have been painted of them, for there is no brighter or more varied costume existing, and the grace and frequently the beauty of the women is beyond question.[116]

A *lawan*, embroidered band for the bottom of a woman's skirt, 320 × 8.5 cm, *c*. 1980. Maiwa collection.

In 1893, Mullaly was appointed as the 'first honourary superintendent of ethnography for Madras presidency'.[117] The man who set up the post was the controversial British official, H. H. Risley.

Census data depended on categories of caste, race and tribe. These were in no way fixed concepts. Some administrators such as Denzil Ibbetson and William Crooke saw caste as largely occupational and social, almost like belonging to a hereditary trade union or guild. Others viewed caste as an institution of Hinduism that was static in nature and fixed through the ages. Administrators such as J. A. Baines and H. H. Risley, however, claimed that the origin of the caste system was, in fact, racial difference. It was this rationale that justified connecting criminality to an entire caste. It was also opined that it was the inherent divisions in caste, divisions that were racial, that made Indian nationalism untenable (they can never unite) and justified British hegemony (we are already united). But Risley went further: he became convinced that caste endogamy had preserved race differences that could be physically measured. Such measurements would give a scientific foundation for ordering castes and tribes into their natural hierarchy of privilege. From high caste to low caste to outcast to tribal, the natives could be measured anthropometrically and ranked in order of status. In 1899, Risley was selected as the commissioner for the 1901 census. Officers were instructed to collect, in addition to statistical data, ethnographic descriptions and anthropometric measurements.[118]

Risley was assisted in his great project by another British ethnographer: Edgar Thurston. The author of the seven-volume set *Castes and Tribes of Southern India* (1909), Thurston was a doctor and superintendent of the Government Museum at Madras (the same museum founded by Edward Balfour in 1850). Thurston took advantage of his position as superintendent to measure museum visitors:

> A visit to the Government Museum at Madras was always a pleasant experience, although at first alarming. Such was [Thurston's] zeal for anthropometry, that he seized every man, woman, and child in order to measure them.[119]

Nicholas Dirks, in his work *Castes of Mind*, offers additional unsettling anecdotes about Thurston, including his weighing local tribesmen using the scales in a butcher shop and his lamenting that 'The Paniyan women of the Wynaad' ran away when they saw him 'believing that I was going to have the finest specimens among them stuffed for the museum. Oh that this were possible!'[120]

Members of criminalized tribes were also measured as part of the identification process. Thurston went to great lengths to train and instruct the police on how to use the expensive and finicky equipment. Fortunately, as a mechanism for criminal identification, anthropometric measurements were replaced by the far less complex (and less racist) practice of fingerprinting, a process initially developed in Bengal at the close of the century.

Thurston's *Castes and Tribes of Southern India* is an extensive work that includes a lengthy description of the Banjara and one melancholy image of two Banjara women. It cites a great deal of previously published information in addition to elements that Thurston received through correspondence. It also contains field work personally undertaken by Thurston himself:

Plate from Edgar Thurston's *Castes and Tribes of Southern India* showing the Lambādi. The photograph was taken before 1908. Stitching on the skirt of the woman on the right indicates these Banjara women are from northern Maharashtra.

Lambadi women often have elaborate tattooed patterns on the backs of the hands, and a tattooed dot on the left side of the nose may be accepted as a distinguishing character of the tribe in some parts. My assistant once pointed out that, in a group of Lambadis, some of the girls did not look like members of the tribe. This roused the anger of an old woman, who said 'You can see the tattoo marks on the nose, so they must be Lambadis.'[121]

The seven volumes give the impression of exhaustive research and encyclopedic authority. Yet it is an unsettling text that remains difficult for the critical reader to trust. The connection between ethnography and criminality continues to haunt descriptions of the Banjara to this day, from Michael Kennedy's 400-page *Notes on Criminal Classes in the Bombay Presidency* published in 1908, up to

M. Krishnamurthy's *Crimes and Customs among the Lambanis in Chitradurga District* published in 2000.

Thurston's 1909 work was perhaps the most ambitious attempt to catalogue the inhabitants of a particular area. There would be other multi-volume works, including tribes and castes catalogues for Bengal (1891), the North-West Provinces and Oudh (1896), Cochin (1909), the Punjab (1916), the Central Provinces (1916), the Nizam's Dominions (1920), Mysore (1928), Travancore (1937) and Coorg (1948).

An attempt at a photographic compendium was made in 1875 with the publication of the eight-volume set *The Peoples of India*. It contains three photographs of interest: one labelled *Brinjaries*, one *Lambani Woman* and one titled *Brinjara and Wife*. As with other ethnographic works, colonial pretext and the construction of criminality colour the reading. To a modern reader it comes across as 'a mixture of gossip, ethnography and military intelligence report, with little attempt at distance or objectivity.'[122] The large volumes were costly to produce and a lukewarm reception by the public discouraged further efforts.[123]

MODERN LIFE

By the close of the nineteenth century, the Banjara had adopted multiple strategies for survival. Large numbers settled down to a permanent residence but still travelled to supply labour for road construction and seasonal harvests. Many became landowners and agriculturalists while others diversified or slowly drifted to urban centres – a trend that would gain momentum after partition in 1947.

A Banjara family travelling by ox cart, Haliyal, Karnataka, 1983.

Migrations with oxen continued on a reduced scale and subject to favourable economic conditions. Anthropologists such as C. H. Childers, who did field work with the Banjara at the close of the 1960s, offer insight into the changing nature of Banjara life. Childers worked with groups who had a permanent residence in central Maharashtra and who migrated to the Western Ghats as far as north Konkan (near Mumbai). They used bullocks loaded with grain in the manner of their ancestors. Childers observed that the Banjara had many ways to avoid rousing the suspicion of neighbouring communities. Members of the same Banjara family would give different names:

> Lamans do not appear among the peoples in the Konkan as a homogeneous group. Whatever their kinship or social ties in home tandas, they appear in the Western Ghats as Bull Lamans, Bullock Seths or contractors, as Woodcutter Lamans, and as Charcoal Seths. The relations of each of these categories with local peoples is different. They also interact very differently among themselves than when at home, even when they are members of the same family.[124]

Childers had the rare privilege of observing the Banjara's preparations for migration. He noted that unlike most nomads they took no tents with them. He also noted that migration was an important rite; one that was significant for self-identification relative to the group:

> Two days before leaving, all things that are to be carried on the trek must be brought out of the house and stacked in the standard camp form, in complete readiness for departure. All those who are to make the journey must sleep outside with the goods, in order to familiarize themselves with conditions and problems. The vessels to be taken are used for cooking, eating, and water storage and no one is supposed to go back in the house for any purpose. Sleeping arrangements are made, the goods are examined and the bullocks loaded to see what things must or can be eliminated or what else is needed. At least one woman and two men are required for every ten or fifteen bullocks.[125]

In northern India, instead of maintaining caravans, the Banjara would purchase oxen and drive them to areas where there was a scarcity in order to sell them. Writing in 1896, William Crooke observed: 'Cattle are largely bred along the Jumna in the direction of Agra and Mathura. These are bought up by the Banjaras, who drive them in large herds to great distances about the time when the agricultural seasons are commencing.' Crooke further observed that they sold to the farmers on credit, returning at harvest time to collect payment. If not paid in a timely fashion, the Banjara did not resort to the law courts but practised a form of coercion known as *dharna*, which consisted of camping out on the debtor's land and verbally harassing them. Crooke reports that: 'This form of pressure appears to be effective with even the most callous debtor, and it is understood that they generally succeed in realizing their money.'[126]

Railways were not economically feasible for the transport of draft animals due to the cost of fodder and water for the long journey. Instead, Banjara men would purchase a third-class ticket to the site where they bought cattle and then walk

Prime Minister Indira Gandhi in traditional Banjara costume, 1983. Indira Gandhi compared the Banjara to golden threads: 'The weavers weave the cloth with golden threads here or there. This adds beauty. Similarly the Lambanis are like the golden thread in the rich Indian cultural heritage.'[127]

beside the herds as they drove them to the melas where the oxen would be sold. The women and children no longer went on these journeys, instead remaining in the tanda while the men travelled.

Through field study, Robert Gabriel Varady noted how this situation changed again after partition. 'Between 1950 and 1954 the "long platform" or "LP" truck was introduced in the subcontinent. Reaction was immediate – Banjaras and other animal dealers quickly noticed the increased capacity of these vehicles.' Varady goes on to describe how a small group of Banjaras could lease a vehicle to provide 'mela to mela' service. The flexibility of routing and the increased size made the trucks economically viable. Varady interviewed a number of Banjara men in the late 1970s. Many remarked on the difference between driving oxen along the open road and using the large trucks: 'In the old days we could work a month and relax for six' one observed, while another commented, 'it was comfortable by foot, and life was cheaper then.' Other interviewees commented how it was now possible for anyone to deal in cattle.[128] A full 100 years after the introduction of railways to India, the remarkable fortitude of those who could undertake long-distance cattle driving was no longer needed.

WHO ARE THE BANJARA?

In 1869, the same year that Mahatma Gandhi was born, N. F. Cumberlege wrote that the accelerating force of modernity must necessarily displace the Banjara.

> Neither their trade nor their tribal system can survive another generation of English predominance, wherefore some account of their more striking peculiarities has at least the interest that attaches to a picture of things which we shall never see again.[129]

This common sentiment has proved untrue. And while it may be tempting to see the collision of Banjara and British cultures as a struggle in which the Banjara are hopelessly outgunned, it must be remembered that the British as a ruling power left India in 1947, while the Banjara persist throughout the country, living in many cases as they always have.

Nevertheless, the question of identity is a profound one. While colonial forces drastically reshaped India's cultural contours, they were but the advance wave of modernity itself. And if rumours of Banjara demise were greatly exaggerated, they still threw the question of identity, in particular, visual identity, into key relief.

The criminalization of tribes combined with the elimination of viable livelihoods served to marginalize and impoverish vast numbers of people. The damage wrecked on tribal identity went deep and had far-reaching consequences. In North America, forced assimilation took the route of criminalizing the markers of tribal identity. Ceremonies and dances such as the West Coast Potlatch and the Tamanawas were outlawed in Canada in 1884.[130] Residential schools worked to dissociate children from their language, customs and beliefs. In India the process was reversed. Customs were largely left alone and the people themselves were criminalized. Following this reversal it can be seen how, in an effort to assuage

OPPOSITE
Despite their reputation as a wandering tribe, many Banjara settlements are now well over a hundred years old. Kendur tanda near Badami is one of these. Shanthavva Lamani sits on the porch of her home, which is made of substantial timbers and features a carved and painted wooden threshold.

Empire of the Caravan | 83

THIS PAGE
Front and back of a bag worked
in brick stitch, 15 cm square,
c. 1980. Maiwa collection.

OPPOSITE
Embroidered cloth composed
of four belt pieces sewn
together; cross stitch and brick
stitch with cotton thread on
cotton backing, 27 × 62 cm,
Maharashtra, *c.* 1940. Maiwa
collection.

the stigma of criminality and escape its effects (poverty, alcoholism, abuse), some felt that the only way forward was to break with tribal identity and merge with mainstream society.

In the 1920s, the group Banjara Jagarana Andolan (Banjara Awakening Movement) was formed. It had several goals but central to its inception was the unification of Banjara culture and, in an effort to improve living conditions, a focus on cleanliness and the elimination of alcohol abuse. But one of its key tenants was also a prohibition against traditional dress for women. As Banjara historian Bhangya Bhukya states in *Subjugated Nomads*, 'The Andolan activists felt that the Lambada were looked down in society because of their women's dress and that it should be discarded.' As the most prominent visual marker of Banjara culture, a woman's choice of clothing thus became contested territory. The choice announced tensions between individual and group identity and between traditional and modern values. Interestingly, women's dress was also transformed from a source of individual and group pride to a sign of coercion. The Andolans 'also preached that caste Hindus compelled [Banjara] women to dress thus in order to subordinate and exploit them.'[131] The reverse might also be true – the attempt to eliminate the costume was, in fact, an attempt to weaken the culture. It was in no way a simple matter.

For traditionalists, to adopt alternate modes of dress such as the sari was to give in to Sanskritization: that is, to adopt the dress and manner of the Hindu majority and to betray the essential qualities of strength and independence that made Banjara special. Many feared that by following this path they would weaken, loose their sense of identity and eventually fade away.

For those who hoped to join mainstream society, however, traditional dress marked them as backwards and brought about discrimination and prejudice. Moving beyond tribal identity prepared them to take part in the modern world, with its promise of education, employment and a better quality of life. Renunciation of tribal values was a mechanism to ascend to higher status.

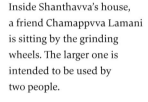

Inside Shanthavva's house, a friend Chamappvva Lamani is sitting by the grinding wheels. The larger one is intended to be used by two people.

Deep inside the house is the kitchen. Beside the hearth Shanthavva demonstrates making roti in a marble dish. Also in the kitchen is an alcove containing the family shrine.

Personal choice of clothing was thus viewed as a fracture between a life of hardship that was rich with cultural tradition on the one hand and a more secure existence purchased at the expense of history and community on the other. But even to set up this dichotomy is to repeat, in another register, the colonial enterprise of controlling identity through definition. It would be misguided, therefore, to equate authenticity with appearance. Take, for example, the case of Banjara men who have never enjoyed a distinctive traditional costume. Their participation in Banjara culture has no sartorial foundation and hence for these members of the tribe, identity is independent of clothing.

There is, moreover, a tendency for cultural outsiders to equate appearance with authenticity. Only women who dress traditionally are 'real' Banjara. This romantic notion also traps tribal cultures in a double bind where, to be legitimate, they are expected to conform to a tribal stereotype: they are not expected to own phones or use computers, drive cars, or dress in a modern style.

There are, however, groups who have successfully navigated the strong currents of tradition and modernity, and even instances of groups re-articulating, in a modern setting, a preference for traditional dress. These groups generally work in handcraft and are skilled in traditional techniques. Makers have become the family's primary wage-earners. Economic advancement redefines a pride in traditional identity while such groups also enjoy advancement in education and quality of life that comes with secure employment. Examples of these groups are the weaving communities of Cusco, Peru, and some of the tribal embroiderers of the Kachchh Desert in western Gujarat. Such groups decide for themselves under what conditions they will adopt traditional dress and how much of it they will maintain. The key point here is that clothing continues to mark cultural distinctions because they have value. Festivals and ceremonies are an opportunity to re-emphasize cultural identity. Dress is not adopted as one would a factory uniform or a costume for historic re-enactment (put on when a visitor arrives and taken off when they leave) – rather clothing is a component of a living tradition.

Ultimately, the world will change and the Banjara will change with it. The real question is: how the Banjara will define who they are and what values they will take with them into the future. Perhaps they will make a path for themselves through the fraught terrain of cultural identity – just as they always have. Perhaps traditional dress for women will not be cast aside as a marker of backwardness but neither will its absence be viewed as a betrayal. Its presence or absence will slip between contesting forces just as the caravans once slipped between warring armies. By taking renewed control of all the elements of tribal identity, the ultimate victors will be now, as in the past, neither of the conflicting armies but the Banjara themselves.

RIGHT

Somlibai's tanda, Malavagoppa, as it appeared in *The Mysore Tribes and Castes*. The photograph was taken some time before 1927 and, below, Malavagoppa as it looked in 2014.

OPPOSITE

Somlibai, an elder in Malavagoppa tanda, is 95 years old. She has lived through many changes, including the partition of India in 1947 and the arrival in her village over 20 years ago of Western anthropologists interested in Banjara embroidery. She still dresses as a Banjara, although she does not wear her full ornament every day. Her two grand-daughters helped her to prepare for this photograph and insisted she wear her full costume.

3 EMBROIDERY
Song of the Cloth

I will be as obedient as thread in the needle...

BANJARA *DEVOLO* (WEDDING SONG)

FOLK EMBROIDERY

In the cultural vault that is India there are embroideries that were made for royal patronage, destined to be given and re-given at court to solicit favour or obligation; there are embroideries made as items of trade, intended for the foreign markets in Arabia and later Europe, and there are folk embroideries made for domestic use, functional or ceremonial and ornamented through a needleworker's skill to please the eye and lift the spirit. Banjara work is folk embroidery. Historically, it was made only for personal use, but it has recently shifted its nature to that of an item of trade. It is often remarked that the mobile nature of the Banjara tanda meant that works were not decorative. There were no wall hangings or bedspreads. Rather, all embroideries were made during, and needed to be useful for, a wandering life.[1]

The fierce pride of the Banjara is also expressed in their stitch work. A sense of this attitude may be found in an encounter between a few Banjara women from Madhya Pradesh and a group of missionaries:

> Some fifty years ago [*c.* 1920] a group of European missionaries wanted a band of Banjaras to settle down and send the young girls to mission schools. The Banjaras maintained that their girls had no need of reading and writing and asked what else the missionaries could teach them to help them to make good wives. The missionaries replied that they taught needlework – it should be mentioned that the needlework taught in missionary institutes in India had attained a high reputation. The Banjaras promptly demanded to see a few specimens of such work and, after inspecting them carefully, turned down the offer, stating that with such unskillful work no Banjara girl could ever hope to find a husband.[2]

But high-quality embroidery skills are not necessary to satisfy the tourist market. In the second half of the twentieth century, the growing international airline industry made India a viable tourist destination. By the 1960s, Goa, Hampi and other tourist centres became places where the Banjara could sell old embroideries and gain income through street performances and divination. When, in the 1980s, a glut of cheap, mass-produced clothing reached India, many abandoned traditional dress. At the same time, economic conditions encouraged a move to the cities where traditional clothing was often dropped. Writing in 1988, Joss Graham, a dealer in ethnic textiles located in London, observed:

> A large quantity of brightly coloured, vegetable dyed, geometric embroidery made by Banjara groups in south India recently appeared on the market. This is a result of these once proud people forgoing their inheritance and migrating to the cities where they shed their exotic costume and trappings.[3]

LEFT
A tailor, whose studio is a table on the street, puts together a Banjara *kachali* using a treadle sewing machine. Strips of mirrors arrive already machine-stitched to fabric backing. Likewise, lines of white beads are pre-assembled into rows. The tailor can attach such items with a few quick stitches, Devarakonda, Telangana, 2014.

BELOW
A cart selling tourist-quality embroidery at the Hampi temple complex. Note the large stitches and abandonment of traditional colour palette and designs, Hampi, Karnataka, 2005.

OPPOSITE
Sitabai adds some additional stitches to her *chhatya* while sitting on her front porch in Maramanahalli tanda, Karnataka, 2013.

Worldwide over-production of clothing and the resultant markets for donations and cast-offs (known in some places as 'dead white man's clothes') has worked to the detriment of many indigenous cultures including the Banjara. In the 1970s and 1980s complete costumes and exquisitely worked pieces came on the market at a relatively low cost. In a short time, however, prices increased and fewer, less impressive pieces were available. In response, dealers cut larger works into smaller pieces and sold them as fragments. At the close of the millennium, two trends were observed: historic pieces were rare and new low-quality works began to be produced to satisfy a tourist demand for ethnic textiles.

Although declining in number, Banjara women continue to make and wear traditional dress. The materials used constantly evolve and change based on what is appealing and what is available. Where there are large numbers of Banjara, local tailors have started to make blouses and skirts. Strips of mirrors and beads can be purchased pre-made and are attached with a few stitches. Such innovation has had a considerable impact on the aesthetic and quality of Banjara clothing.

STITCHWORK

Banjara work is caught between accepting and rejecting outside influence. Constant mobility brought Banjara into contact with many cultures, however, self-reliance led them to reject most stylistic change. Their itinerant nature, together with their reluctance to reveal too much information about themselves, explains the dearth of textile provenance. The problem is compounded by the fact that the Indian merchants who gathered textiles either did not collect source information or else withheld it to protect their market. Some generalizations still hold, though, and to this day, Banjara embroidery almost never contains figurative motifs such as flowers, animals, or human forms. The exception to this is the Khandesh area, where zoomorphic imagery was occasionally rendered in brick or cross stitch.

London dealer Joss Graham characterized Banjara embroidery as 'pre-Mughal' in that it eschews the floral and vine motifs favoured for frames and backgrounds in Mughal art and architecture.[4] The extent to which Banjara work was influenced by the Mughals is, of course, very difficult to say. Almost all Banjara pieces in both private and public collections were made in the twentieth century with only a few items surviving from the late nineteenth century. Yet there is a clear sense in which the term pre-Mughal emphasizes Banjara independence and effectively separates their design sense from the plethora of more figurative embroidery traditions.

Few groups deploy the variety of stitches used by the Banjara. Of the many stitches used, counted stitchwork – consisting of brick and cross stitch worked on the weave of the ground fabric – stands out as unique. Such work is found in northern Maharashtra and the southern part of Madhya Pradesh in an area that is roughly the historic region of Khandesh. This style is easily worked on coarse weaves but on finer fabrics it can resemble weaving. The fabric remains quite flexible. With cross-stitch imagery there is a predominance of chequerboard

Front and back of a brick-stitched envelope bag. This type of bag is identical to Hazara work from Jaghori (Ghazni) in the collection of the Musée du Quai Branly in Paris. The bag shown is 15 cm square when closed, *c.* 1930. Maiwa collection.

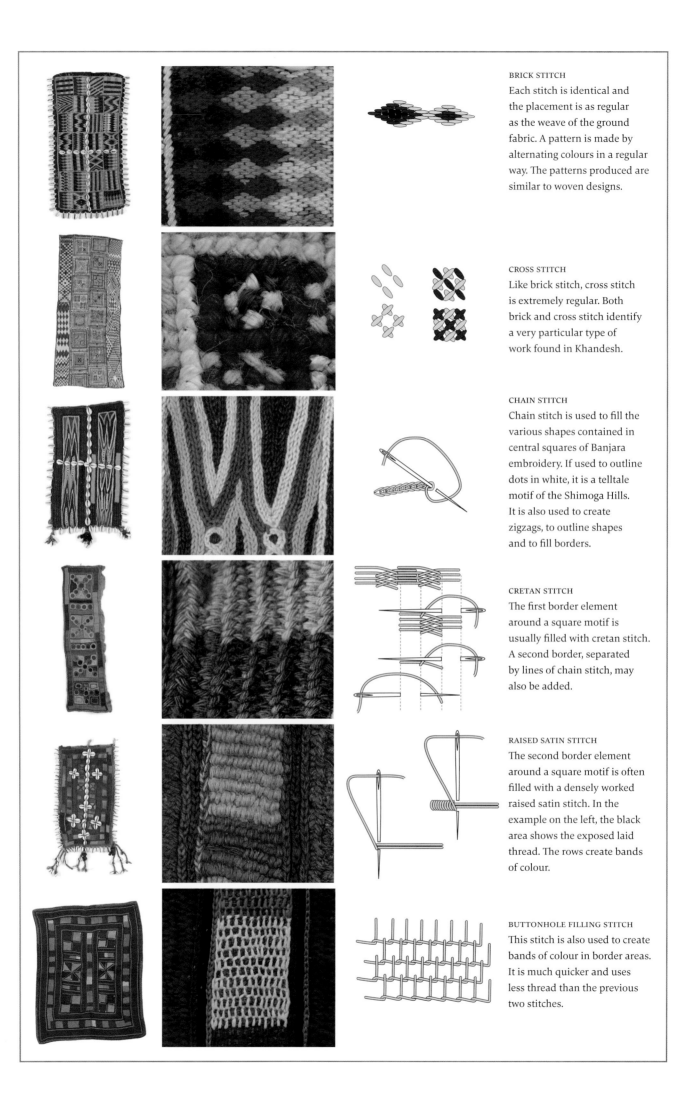

BRICK STITCH

Each stitch is identical and the placement is as regular as the weave of the ground fabric. A pattern is made by alternating colours in a regular way. The patterns produced are similar to woven designs.

CROSS STITCH

Like brick stitch, cross stitch is extremely regular. Both brick and cross stitch identify a very particular type of work found in Khandesh.

CHAIN STITCH

Chain stitch is used to fill the various shapes contained in central squares of Banjara embroidery. If used to outline dots in white, it is a telltale motif of the Shimoga Hills. It is also used to create zigzags, to outline shapes and to fill borders.

CRETAN STITCH

The first border element around a square motif is usually filled with cretan stitch. A second border, separated by lines of chain stitch, may also be added.

RAISED SATIN STITCH

The second border element around a square motif is often filled with a densely worked raised satin stitch. In the example on the left, the black area shows the exposed laid thread. The rows create bands of colour.

BUTTONHOLE FILLING STITCH

This stitch is also used to create bands of colour in border areas. It is much quicker and uses less thread than the previous two stitches.

RUNNING STITCH

Used to quilt together layers of fabric for the construction of bags. It results in a very durable cloth.

RUNNING STITCH VARIATIONS

A pattern is created by changing the colour of threads used for the running stitch, or varying their placement. The zigzag is a common feature on quilted cloth.

INTERLACING

The even placement of running stitches provides an excellent grid to anchor additional threads. This interlacing forms distinctive patterns that may be used as borders, lines, or as elements in larger patterns.

MAAKI STITCH

The pattern formed by interlacing is sometimes called *maaki*. It is reproduced by this stitch, which is a triangle with a twisted tail.

HERRINGBONE

Herringbone, closed herringbone and herringbone with couching on the crosses.

BUTTONHOLE STITCH

This stitch is used as a linear element, to finish the edges of a piece, or, when worked in a circle, as a substitute for a mirror.

LEFT

Stitches used on prestige pieces. These stitches are worked for maximum density and are intended to completely cover the base fabric.

OPPOSITE

Stitches used to quilt multiple layers of fabric together. These stitches leave the base fabric visible and act almost as line drawings on the cloth surface.

patterning and the liberal use of the quincunx. The brick-stitch work displays patterning that is familiar to weaving traditions: lozenges, checks, zigzags and diagonals. Banjara brick-stitch work is similar to the work of Hazara embroiderers from central Afghanistan. A number of small envelope bags in the collection of the Musée du Quai Branly in Paris are identical in terms of both stitch and pattern to Banjara pieces.[5] The similarity might be evidence that Banjara migrated from

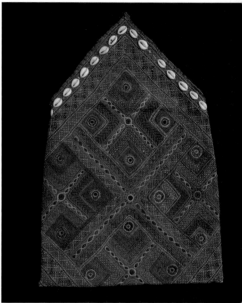

India through Afghanistan during an early exodus. Alternatively, the influence could be more recent – brought back when the Banjara were commissariat for an Afghan campaign.

In contrast to the dense, ground-covering embroidery on page 96, much of the stitching on quilted bags is open, revealing the ground fabric. The structural component of quilting is the running stitch. This stitch anchors two or more cloths together and results in a very durable and long-lasting construction. Basic variations in this work play with the position or colour of the running stitch itself, or use the regular gridwork of these stitches to add interlacing. In addition to the central running stitches, other embellishments such as chain stitch, buttonhole wheels, brick-stitch lozenges and so on will be added. These stitches only go through the top layer. Quality in such work is not in the complexity of the stitches but in their execution.

ABOVE LEFT AND TOP
A quilted bag made from block-printed fabric. Considerable care has been taken with the seams and running stitches, *c.* 1900. Maiwa collection.

ABOVE AND OPPOSITE
A quilted bag with exceptionally fine interlacing stitches, Shimoga Hills, *c.* 1920. John Childs collection.

PATTERN

In contrast to the stitchwork of Khandesh, the embroidery of the Shimoga Hills and much of Karnataka is built up of geometric elements that are independent of the stitches used to make them. Squares are subdivided into equilateral triangles and right triangles and these are filled with rows of chain stitch. Shapes may be filled with concentric rows, layers of rows, zigzag lines, or (when filling a square) a series of right angles that decrease in size as they move away from the centre. Shapes may be varied through the addition of central crosses, either on the diagonal, or perpendicular to the containing figure. The centre of such a figure is a source of power and hence a choice location for a mirror or buttonhole wheel. These basic patterns may be nested, repeated, or scaled to fill space. Such squares, when augmented by border elements, fit the basic rectangular shapes that comprise all of the Banjara's traditional cloth. The shapes of bags are a natural result of this quadratophelia. Such patterning is often apprehended unconsciously: a person can identify a Banjara embroidery without being able to say exactly what it is that makes it Banjara. The reverse is also true. Deviation from these pattern principles is often the first tip-off that a piece is not Banjara.

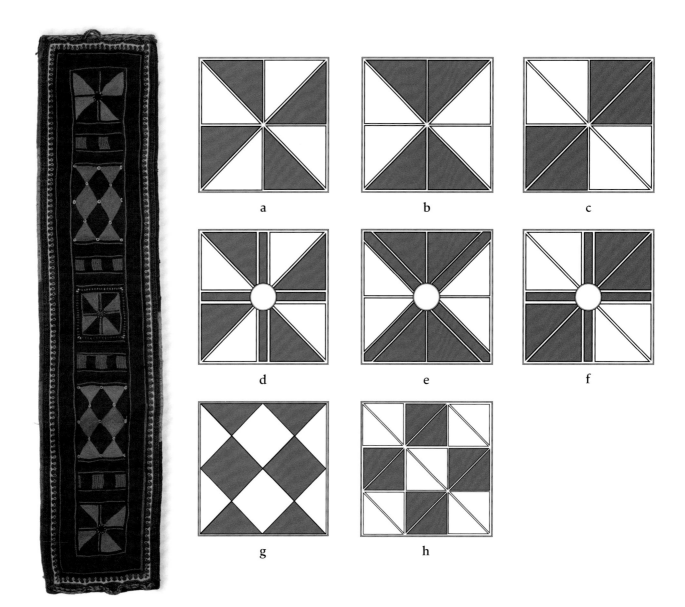

Another distinctive design element is deliberate symmetry breaking. A mirror will be added, seemingly at random, to a composition, or a pattern will be asymmetric in colour or form. To the casual observer it sometimes looks as if the embroiderer ran out of the right-coloured thread or was not paying attention to the composition. However, closer examination shows that such elements are quite wilful and never added in such a place as to justify a lack of materials. The Banjara believe, as many cultures do, that a perfect creation is an act of hubris, inviting divine retribution. The way the embroiderers break symmetry without contravening their natural design sense shows a high level of creativity.

The preponderance of the square in embroidery is difficult to explain, especially as it is not found in other groups originating in north-west India. It could be that at some point in their history the figure became associated with a protective influence. Edgar Thurston collected the following anecdote from Hayavandana Rao, who travelled from Jeypore to Malkangiri with the Banjara:

> They regard themselves as immune from the attacks of tigers if they take certain precautions. Most of them have to pass through places infested with these beasts, and their favourite method of keeping them off is as follows. As soon as they encamp at a place, they level a square bit of ground, and light fires in the middle of it, round which they pass the night. It is their firm belief that the tiger will not enter the square, from fear lest it should become blind and eventually be shot.[6]

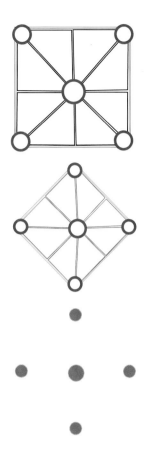

ABOVE

Mirror placement based on the vertices of the square. The same figure turned 45° is an auspicious tattoo marking placed on the chin and the temple. It appears to be one of the few embroidery motifs that is also found marked on the skin.

LEFT

A quilted square based on the modified check of nine squares (below), 60 cm sq, *c.* 1930. Maiwa collection.

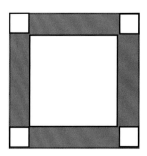

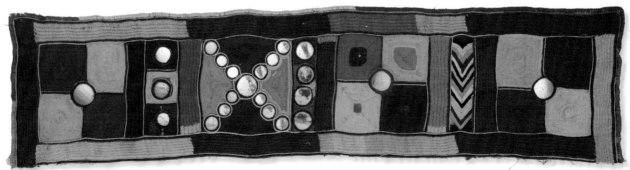

MIRRORWORK

PREVIOUS PAGES
LEFT
Embroidered *pulia*; most embroideries follow a similar order in stitching the figure. The central squares are worked in chain stitch, the first band is filled with cretan stitch and the second band is filled with rows of raised satin stitch, *c.* 1940. Maiwa collection.

LEFT BELOW
Part of an embroidered waistband for a woman's skirt. The squares are filled with tight rows of chain stitch and embellished with hand-blown mirrors. Worked in the dominant Banjara colours of red, yellow and orange, the piece is asymmetric yet balanced.

RIGHT
Embroidered *pulia* worked in a very neat style, *c.* 1980. Maiwa collection.

BELOW
Mirrors are also known as *shisha*. Below is the *shisha* stitch used to secure the mirror to fabric. The mirror is first held in place with a network of anchor stitches. The *shisha* stitch ties the anchor stitches to the base cloth. There are several variations on the *shisha* stitch.

Mirrors used in tribal embroidery are traditionally made from hand-blown artisan glass. Artisans in Kapadvanj, Gujarat, are still producing mirrors using a method first developed by the ancient Romans. A *shishger* (mirror-maker) starts with a ball of red-hot glass. He blows it into a large, fine bulb of exceptional size – usually 50 centimetres in diameter. The sphere is detached from the blowpipe and a molten mixture of zinc and lead is poured inside. These metals fuse to the glass and provide 'silver', which is the reflective surface.

Once cool, the spheres are carefully broken and the resulting shards trimmed into a variety of shapes with special scissors. The mirrors are sorted by passing them through a series of sieves before being graded and priced.

Handmade glass has many imperfections: bubbles, lines and cracks. However, it is thinner and lighter than the glass that can be obtained from breaking contemporary mirrors. The irregularities add character and are much sought after by embroiderers. The tendency of these mirrors to turn darker as the metals oxidize, together with imperfections in the glass itself, has led to them being referred to as 'black glass'. The embroidery market is also supplied with ready-cut mirrors in a variety of shapes. As with trimming contemporary mirrors, these pieces tend to be thicker. The perfect uniformity of such pieces is not always desired.

The rationale for the use of mirrors is consistent across many tribal communities – they are primarily auspicious and defensive. Mirrors ward off the evil eye, reflecting it back on the sender. Different tribal communities prefer different sizes and shapes. The Gracia Jat and Mutwa of the Kachchh region prefer tiny mirrors, which they place inside a network of complex geometric patterns. Banjara taste tends towards large mirrors, which complement their bold geometric patterns. Regional variations are evident: in northern Karnataka, the sleeves of a woman's *choli* use circular mirrors augmented by buttons, whereas closer to Hyderabad the sleeve is covered with rectangular pieces, embellished with white beads.

The placement of mirrors on embroidery is very important because of the power they have. Mirrors are placed at the centre of designs as in the nexus of a spider's web. The Banjara also use them in a quincunx pattern. Notably, if mirrors are unavailable, distinctive stitches will fill the place where the mirror should be, thus maintaining the pattern and a place of importance. The Banjara occasionally use a variety of mirrors of different sizes to fill an area of cloth. The seemingly random distribution on the field is remarkable and is unlike any other embroidery tradition. Thin metal buttons are a recent addition to embroideries. Placement seems to suggest that they have the same role as beads and other embellishments, and that they do not carry auspicious powers.

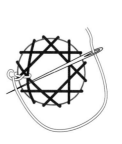

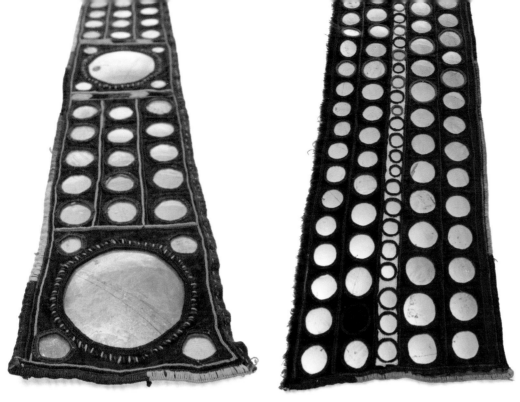

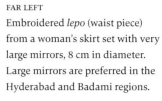

FAR LEFT
Embroidered *lepo* (waist piece) from a woman's skirt set with very large mirrors, 8 cm in diameter. Large mirrors are preferred in the Hyderabad and Badami regions.

LEFT
Mirrored waistband from a skirt. This piece contains over one hundred mirrors made from handblown glass, *c.* 1960, Karnataka. Maiwa collection.

BELOW LEFT
Embroidered bag set with over 300 mirrors. The shoulder strap was not part of the original bag, Shimoga Hills, *c.* 1930. Maiwa collection.

BELOW
The demand of tribal communities for 'black glass' (handmade mirrors) is met by a small group of *shishger* artisans. They produce a large glass ball and silver the inside while it is still hot. Once cool, the ball is carefully broken and then trimmed with special scissors. Decline in the demand for traditional dress has had a severe impact on the livelihood of these specialized artisans.

COWRIES AND COINS

Both cowrie shells (*monetaria moneta*) and coins have the same symbolic role in embroidery, and both were used as currency in India. In the early eighteenth century (a period of relatively stable exchange rates), the value was on average 65 cowries to the paisa. Four paisa made an anna and sixteen anna made a rupee. A seashell may seem a strange currency, but they are difficult to forge and their low value made forgery unlikely. The rarity in the lands where they were used secured their value. They were also uniform and easily identified. In the sixteenth century cowries were supplied to Bengal from the Maldives by the Portuguese and they remained in general circulation for centuries. Tavernier observed the use of cowries throughout India 'close to the sea they give up to 80 for the paisá and that diminishes as you leave the sea on account of carriage so that at Agra you receive but 50 or 55 for the paisá.'[7] In 1807, the British passed a regulation refusing to accept the cowrie for revenue payment. This, combined with inflation and the introduction of low-value copper currency, effectively de-valued the shells and they slowly went out of circulation.

In addition to their value as currency, cowries are considered auspicious and are frequently used to propitiate Laxmi, the goddess of wealth, especially during the festival of Diwali. To this day, 'energized' cowries may be purchased to be kept in offices or places of business (cash boxes are recommended) to bring prosperity and encourage the accumulation of wealth.

Cowries and coins, when combined with stitch work and worn in public, made two prominent aspects of prestige visible – wealth and skill. The addition of the talismanic properties of the mirrors gave embroiderers not only considerable options in the construction of an embroidery, but also a finished object that permeated energy and had the potency to protect the wearer from harm.

LEAD BEADS

Pressed lead beads are found in cowrie florets, cowrie pendants, as collars for pompoms and on their own in tassels. They confirm a delight in weighty ornament, but also have a special role. Nora Fisher observed that:

> The most significant ornaments – ones that signal ethnicity, lineage and community position – are fashioned of simple lead. In the equality minded tanda, the wife of the headman or naik is only very subtly identified by a tiny lead-adorned square embroidered bag. Similarly, the man's amuletic waist string and the woman's dance ornaments are composed only of string, yarn tassels and leaden pieces.[8]

Lead beads are also sewn onto cloth bracelets and anklets. Glass beads and tiny metal balls are popular as well and may frequently be found lining the edge of smaller embroidered bags.

ABOVE
Double strand of cowries with cowrie florets as an ornament on the shoulder strap of a beaded bag, Kadiyala Kunta tanda, 2014.

OPPOSITE ABOVE
Gala used for carrying water with a cowrie net in place of the usual *pulia, c.* 1960. John Childs collection.

OPPOSITE BELOW LEFT
Triple strands of cowries hang from a *pachela*. Made with cloth, lead beads, coin, *c.* 1960. Maiwa collection.

OPPOSITE BELOW RIGHT
Cowrie florets made with cowrie shells and buttons on *dori* (ties from a skirt).

APPLIQUÉ

Large appliqué figures appear in embroideries from the Khandesh region and are another hallmark of the Banjara's north-western origins. Such figures are common on Rajasthan quilts and the Sami quilts from the Sindh region of Pakistan and the Kachchh region of Gujarat. Appliqué work is done over block-printed cotton or on coarse cotton weaves dyed with madder or indigo. The appliqué is created by cutting the figures, turning under the edges and then appliquéing them onto the fabric. In addition to floating figures, appliqué is used to create a fine border of triangles. These appliqué figures are topped with a nakra stitch. This element is often described as a 'temple' figure and is a common motif, especially on quilted bags and skirt borders. When fabric is unavailable, artisans will re-create the triangles with embroidery.

OPPOSITE

A Banjara cloth: the centre is worked in counted brick stitch, framed with embroidery and appliqué, approx. 60 × 90 cm, c. 1960. John Childs collection.

BELOW

Two bags, one with appliqué and one imitating appliqué using embroidery.

RIGHT

An unusual variation on the *kachali* with sleeves made from block-printed cotton, and appliqué figures, c. 1970. Maiwa collection.

4 BANJARA STYLE
Clothing and Ornament

Their dress is peculiar, and their ornaments are so singularly chosen that we have, we are confident, seen women who (not to mention a child at their backs) have had eight or ten pounds weight in metal or ivory round their arms and legs.

EDWARD MOOR, *NARRATIVE OF CAPTAIN LITTLE'S DETACHMENT*, 1794

The Banjara costume is similar to that of other tribal groups originating in Rajasthan. It is comprised of three main elements: a backless blouse known as a *kachali*, which covers the front and is tied at the back with strings; a colourful and voluminous skirt called a *ghagra* or *phetiya*, depending on whether it has a drawstring or includes a wide embroidered waistband (the skirt ends at the lower calf so that the substantial anklets are visible) and a headscarf or *chhatya* that is worn asymmetrically. The longer end of the headscarf is brought under the arm and tucked into the skirt in front. It can hang at the back or completely wrap the torso – either for modesty or as protection against the elements.

Y. Ruplanaik repeats the following legend about the Banjara and their clothing.

There is a legend regarding the Banjara dress. It is aid that during a marriage a bridegroom died all of a sudden after the couple had gone around the sacred fire and the two pestols. Thereupon the bride, while weeping and cursing her fate, tore to pieces all her fine wedding clothes. Goddess parvathi heard her wailings and appealed to shiva to give the vital life again to the bridegroom. Accordingly they appeared on the scene and gave needle and thread to the bride to get all her fine cloths pieced together and at the same time giving back life to the dead bridegroom. Since that day, they say that the Banjara women prepared for themselves the kind of dress that they wear by tearing the new cloth into suitable pieces and sewing them into ghagra (Phetiya) bodice (Kaanchali) veil over the head (Chaantiya) and so on. Hence it is said that they indulge in their gorgeous and fastidious dress.[1]

లంబాడీ వారు

PIECES USED IN THE CONSTRUCTION OF A *KACHALI*

1 *Chhati*: rectangular piece covering the breasts.
2 *Peti*: a piece covering the navel. It sometimes contains a pocket for coins or keys.
3 *Chirma*: a piece covering the sides of the breasts and the ribs.
4 *Khadapa*: a piece hanging below the *chirma*.
5 *Khuppa*: a piece on either side of the neck opening.
6 *Bahi*: short sleeves.
7 *Katta*: piping around the neck opening and the bottom of the garment.
8 *Dari*: strings tied in the middle of the back.
9 *Dori*: strings tied around the neck. These pieces are cut out of coarse *chhatya* cloth and lined on the inside with softer *mangji* fabric.

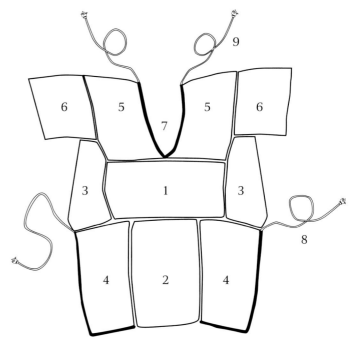

EMBROIDERED BLOUSE (*KACHALI*)

Traditional Banjara clothing is constructed in pieces. Each part is embellished before being combined to form the finished garment. This mode of production is well suited to a life on the move. A woman can keep everything necessary to embroider a section of clothing in a *kothali* (small bag). Not even scissors are needed. As recently as 1981, women were still using the traditional method of cutting the coarse *chhatya* (headscarf) cloth to size with a sharpened sickle.[2]

The *kachali* is a basic structure that has evolved into many regionally distinct variations. The size and placement of the pieces, as well as the method of embellishment, changes from place to place. In Shimoga, for example, the *chhati* (the piece that covers the breasts) is wider and is completely covered in medium-sized mirrors. The *kachali* may be given at marriage and if it is then it will have five additional embroidered flaps attached. The flaps, called *karya*, indicate that a woman is married and must be removed if she is widowed. Flaps above the breasts are called *thinkli*, those above the shoulders, *khariya*, and those above the navel, *peti*.

In the past, the independence and isolation of Banjara tandas meant that the work of piecing together the *kachali* would never be trusted to a tailor. Today, however, there are Banjara tailors who not only piece together the finished garment, but also machine stitch on pre-made decorations such as bands of mirrors, beads and buttons. This recent innovation may account for the uniformity of *kachali* worn in a particular area since they are all the work of the same tailor.

OPPOSITE ABOVE
Kachali with embroidery, mirrors, pom-poms, coins and lead beads, Shimoga Hills, *c.* 1960. Maiwa collection.

BELOW LEFT
Kachali, *c.* 1970, photographed on location in Malavagoppa tanda, Karnataka, 2014.

BELOW RIGHT
The flaps marked in red are *karya*: they indicate that a woman is married and are removed if she is widowed.

OVERLEAF
Two *kachali* from Maharashtra or Madhya Pradesh, *c.* 1980 (right) and 1960 (left). John Childs collection.

SKIRT (*GHAGRA*, *PHETIYA*, *LANGRA*)

Like the blouse, Banjara skirts are made from separate pieces that are embroidered and then sewn together. There can be considerable variations in embroidery style and in the fabrics chosen to make the garment. The *ghagra* is a drawstring skirt without a waistband. The *phetiya* is similar in design but it has an embroidered waistband that covers the midrift. This band is often a showpiece and is so densely embroidered that it will remain intact even when the rest of the garment is in tatters. Both the *ghagra* and *phetiya* are of a length that permits the anklets to remain visible. The *langra* falls lower, is not as wide at the bottom and is less lavishly decorated.

PIECES USED IN THE CONSTRUCTION OF A *PHETIYA*

1 *Lepo*: this piece can be as much as 20 cm in height and is often densely embroidered.
2 *Ghero*: closely pleated or gathered fabric may be made with block-printed *mangji*, usually black and red.
3 *Sabab*: when cotton is used, this area may contain appliqué figures. In Khandesh, *mushru* cloth (a cotton weave weft-faced with silk) is used, however, modern tastes run to silver or gold brocade.
4 *Lawan*: the border at the bottom, which is also embroidered.
5 *Dori*: strings to tie around the waist, which may be augmented by cowries and pom-poms.

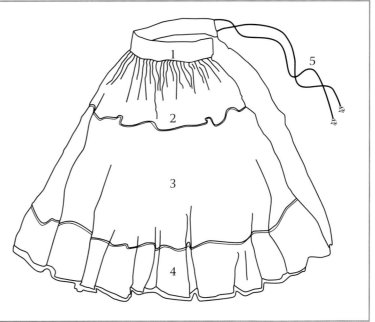

Phetiya, central Karnataka,
c. 1940. Maiwa collection.

Phetiya with embroidered *lepo*,
fine appliqué work and cowries
on the *dori* strings. Badami
region, Karnataka, *c.* 1900.
Maiwa collection.

Phetiya with mirrored *lepo*, bells and beads on the *dori* strings, southern Karnataka, *c.* 1930. Maiwa collection.

A less elaborate *phetiya* made from block-printed cloth, central Karnataka, *c.* 1920. Maiwa collection.

BELOW LEFT
Ghagra with *mushru* cloth and embroidered border, photographed near Maheshwar, Madhya Pradesh, 2014.

BELOW RIGHT
The owner holding her wedding photograph in which she is wearing the skirt shown below.

Ghagra composed of contrasting fabrics. The left side is block-printed cotton with a border dyed with madder and indigo. The right side is *mushru* cloth. The embroidered band indicates that this skirt originates from the Khandesh region. Collection of Laxmi Naik and Jan Duclos. Photographed on location in Kaddirampura, Karnataka, 2013.

LEFT

The centre band of this *ghagra* is synthetic fabric that is designed to resemble traditional *mushru* cloth. Authentic *mushru* cloth is a combination of cotton and silk woven in such a way that the cotton covers most of one side of the cloth. The Koran prohibits wearing silk 'next to the skin' and so the cloth is worn with the cotton side in. It is an ingenious example of weaving technology solving a religious prohibition. *Mushru* cloth is popular among many cultures outside of the Muslim population, photographed near Maheshwar, Madhya Pradesh, 2014.

Sitting on her veranda in the evening light Gumlibai adds running stitch to a piece of fabric that will be used for a skirt. The bangles on her forearm are bone (not plastic), Shimoga Hills, 2014.

Piklibai adds some interlacing stitches to an embroidery, Maramanahalli tanda, 2013.

Sandibai and her daughter on the threshold of her house, Maramanahalli tanda, 2013.

In contrast to the dusty browns of the
land, the Banjara's clothes are a feast
of colour. These women are wearing
elaborately decorated *chhatya*
made from coarse cotton cloth; they
embroider for Sandur Kushala Kala
Kendra, an NGO, Sandur, 2005.

HEADSCARF (CHHATYA)

Throughout most of India, the Banjara headscarf is not worn as a veil – a Banjara woman will almost never hide her face from view. This trait has contributed to the fabled boldness and strength of the women. Another practice that has remained exclusive to the Banjara is the habit of tying a plain headscarf at the back or side in a manner that keeps the hair in place. This style led some to refer to the Banjara as 'Indian gypsies'. The festival *chhatya* has a separate strip of embroidery, often with dense rows of mirrors, attached to frame the face. This strip is called a *gungta* and like the *lepo* on a *phetiya* it is a highly visible showpiece. Occasionally, pendants or *pamdi* are added to the embroidered designs, which fall in the middle of the back.

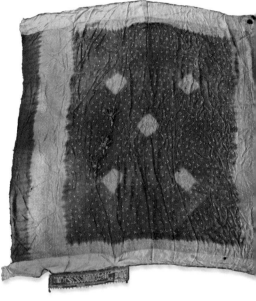

ABOVE
A *chhatya* photographed in Malavagoppa tanda, Karnataka, 2014.

LEFT
Sakuntala, an embroiderer at Surya's Garden, wearing a *chhatya* typical of central Karnataka. Collection of Laxmi Naik and Jan Duclos, 2013.

OVERLEAF
Chavlibai holds up her special *chhatya*, Malavagoppa tanda, Karnataka, 2014.

Clothing and Ornament | 125

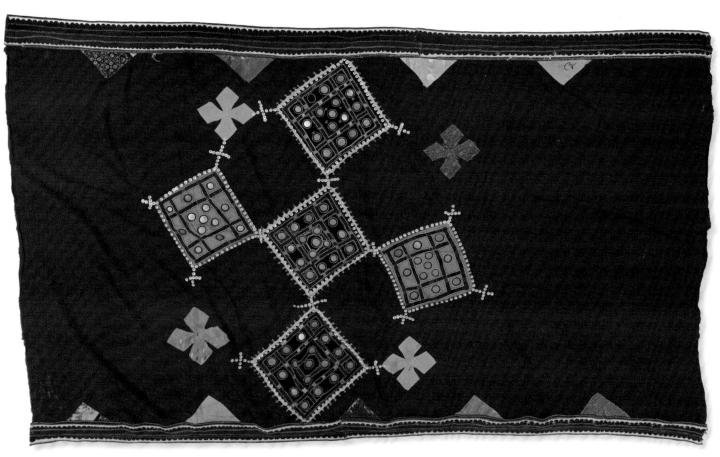

TOP
Chhatya from central or
western Karnataka, *c.* 1940.
Maiwa collection.

ABOVE
Chhatya with mirrors,
embroidery and machine-sewn
appliqué, central Karnataka,
c. 1960. Maiwa collection.

Two *chhatya* with mirrors,
embroidery and machine-sewn
appliqué, central Karnataka,
c. 1960. Maiwa collection.

CHUNDA

One of the more exceptional elements of the Banjara costume is the *chunda*, a stick which is braided into the hair and covered with a headscarf. The length of the *chunda* can range from a few centimetres to over a metre. The length is counterbalanced by a cluster of pom-poms hanging down the back. The *chunda* is only worn by married women and the angle is said to denote a woman's status in the community. By elevating the cloth off the head, women claimed the heat of the sun was reduced. The use of the *chunda* is limited to the Khandesh region and it is not found in the south.

The headdress is reminiscent of the European hennin, which reached its most elaborate form in medieval French courts in the mid-fifteenth century. The Banjara *chunda* also fascinated British ethnographers. In 1918, William Crooke published a monograph speculating on the cultural influences that might have led to its use. In the Khandesh region there is some evidence that up until the 1980s the *chunda* still formed part of a woman's daily costume. Today, this spectacular headdress is only worn on special festive occasions. Preparing the hair and costume for such events is rarely a solitary or solemn activity and it takes hours of women working together to achieve the desired effect.

The short *chunda* is also worn by a group of Rabaris in the far north-west of Rajasthan near Jaisalmer. Women of the Maru Raikas will tie a short stick called a *shing* or *ati* into their hair.[3] This is just one of the many elements that link the Banjara to an ancestral homeland in the Rajput area.

ABOVE
Watercolour of traditional
Banjara dress by M. V.
Dhurandhar, 1928.

ABOVE
Inside the house, a *chunda* is
arranged on the wearer's head
and the *punda* (counterweight),
a cluster of woollen pom-poms,
is braided into her hair.

LEFT
The *chunda* being worn, Masidpura
tanda, Madhya Pradesh, 2014.

OPPOSITE BELOW
Four *chunda* photographed on
location, 2014. From the left:
a wooden *chunda* without a
counterweight, Chiktiyabad tanda,
Maharashtra; an aluminium *chunda*
with rope to be braided into the hair;
a wooden *chunda* with a purse as
punda; a black hardwood *chunda*
with a synthetic woollen pom-pom
punda. They were photographed in
Dhar, Maharashtra, except for the
one on the far left.

Clothing and Ornament | 131

WATER CARRYING

Life in much of India requires a daily trip to the well to fetch water. In the case of the Banjara this task is facilitated through the use of a *gala*, a twisted length of cloth wound with rope to make a ring. A small square of cloth called a *gaadi* is placed on the head over the headscarf, the ring is placed on this cloth and the pot is placed on the ring. The pot is covered with another cloth called a *garna*. Attached to the *gala* and hanging down the back is an elaborately worked piece called a *pulia*. As with other highly visible textiles, the *pulia* is a showpiece designed to exhibit a woman's skill. It is the only Banjara textile of its size that is rectangular. The headdress is often used during the Teej festival, when a basket with newly sprouted wheat is placed on the head.

ARTICLES FOR WATER CARRYING

The arrangement of articles for water carrying, Madakaripura tanda, Karnataka, 2014.

1 *Garna*   3 *Gaadi*
2 *Gala*   4 *Pulia*

OPPOSITE
Pulia embroidered in a number
of styles, showing variations
of the patterns discussed in
the previous chapter. They are
from Karnataka and Telangana,
c. 1910–50. Maiwa collection.

ABOVE
A full ensemble of a *gala*, *gaadi*
and *pulia*, Telangana, *c.* 1960.
Maiwa collection.

RIGHT
A partial ensemble of a *gala*
and *pulia*. The *pulia* has an
outside cowrie border, internal
lines of cowries and each
square element has a pom-pom
with lead beads, Karnataka,
c. 1930. John Childs collection.

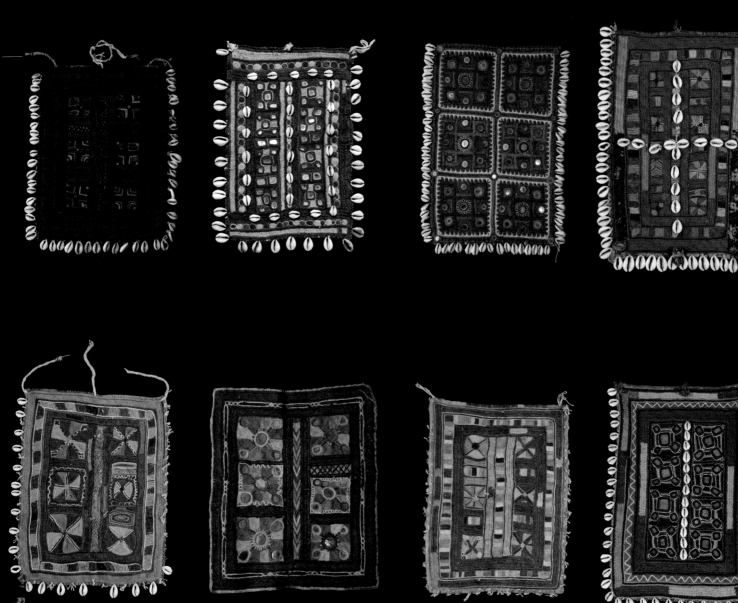
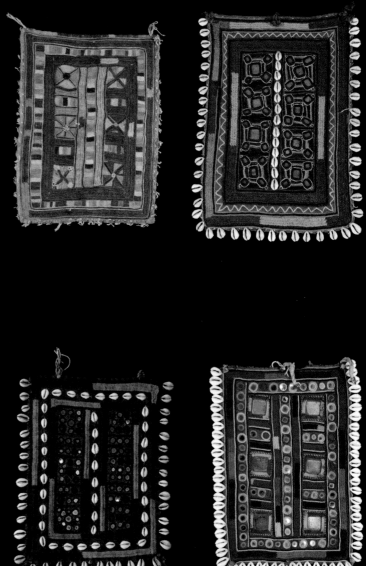
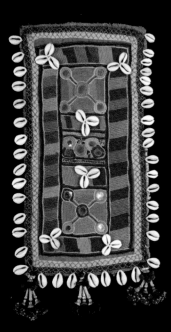
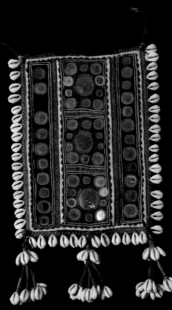

JEWELRY

The line between embroidery, jewelry and clothing is not easily drawn. Garments may be so heavily embellished with mirrors, coins, lead beads and cowries that they almost qualify as jewelry. All items play a similar role in the life of a person and all are designed to communicate status, wealth and prestige, while also protecting the wearer from harm. Embroidery, in particular, is intended to exhibit skill, manual dexterity, suitability for marriage and the ability to partake in adult life. Jewelry, in contrast, is a display of affluence and security. Women and men wear their wealth even while labouring in the fields or on the roads. This makes sense with a peripatetic culture where the most secure place is on your person. It also makes sense in a setting where colour and ornament are very much desired and going into the world unadorned is unthinkable.

As might be expected from the conditions in which jewelry is worn, Banjara ornament tends toward the robust and sturdy. The weight of the ensemble is noteworthy. The skirt, blouse and headscarf alone can weigh 2 to 5 kilos, with the bracelets, anklets, necklaces, waist chains, earrings and other effects weighing an additional 2 to 5 kilos. Much of the jewelry is not bulky, but rather is composed of myriad weighty elements. Hollow lead balls, for example, containing a lead grain that is designed to tinkle while moving, are ubiquitous.

OPPOSITE
Neelavva with a wealth of jewelry, Nagarasakopa tanda, 2013.

BELOW LEFT
Cloth cord necklace with lead beads, bells and a central mirror pendant festooned with beads and bells. Maiwa collection.

BELOW RIGHT
A cloth bracelet with lead beads, lead pendant collars, pom-poms and lac beads. John Childs collection.

RIGHT
A necklace made from a cloth cord with one-rupee coins and a three-pendant centrepiece. Maiwa collection.

BELOW
A wire-wrapped necklace with three pendants worn as a marriage symbol. Such necklaces are not exclusive to the Banjara and are found among a variety of tribal communities in Gujarat. Maiwa collection.

BELOW RIGHT
Solid silver necklace, *hansuli*, photographed in Dhar, Madhya Pradesh, 2014.

OPPOSITE
A chain necklace, *rupaya har*, festooned with rupee coins, photographed on location in Chiktiyabad tanda, Karnataka, 2014.

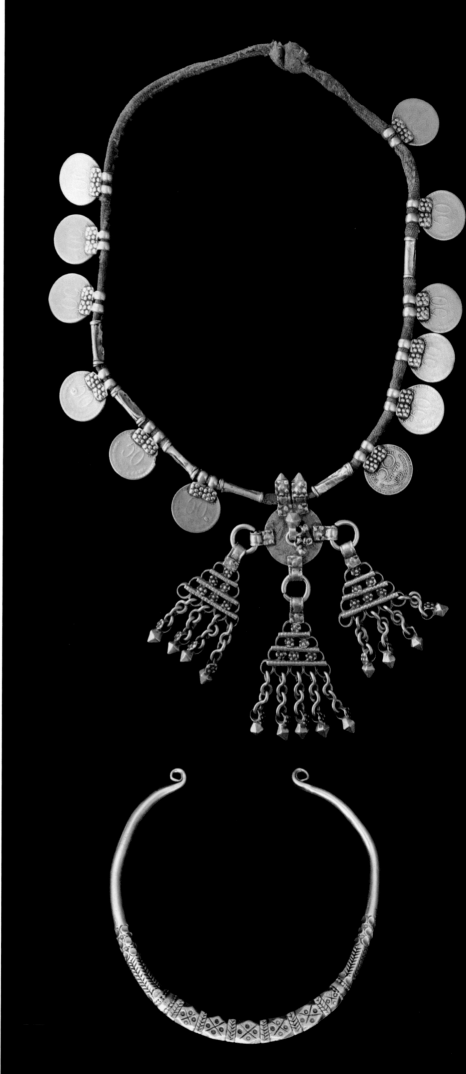

RIGHT ABOVE

An essential part of Banjara jewelry, these hollow bell-shaped pendant *topli* are worn by braiding the cord into the hair. In Telangana they are worn next to the temple, while in Karnataka they are worn lower down at the level of the chin.

RIGHT BELOW

Pressed metal buttons are part of the *topli* and worn just above the pendants. These are also hollow and filled with madder-dyed sheep's wool.

BELOW

Braiding hair is invariably done in pairs. It is a social occasion between mother and daughter or between close friends, Karnataka, 2013.

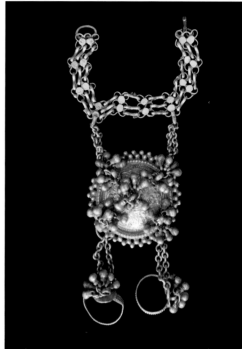

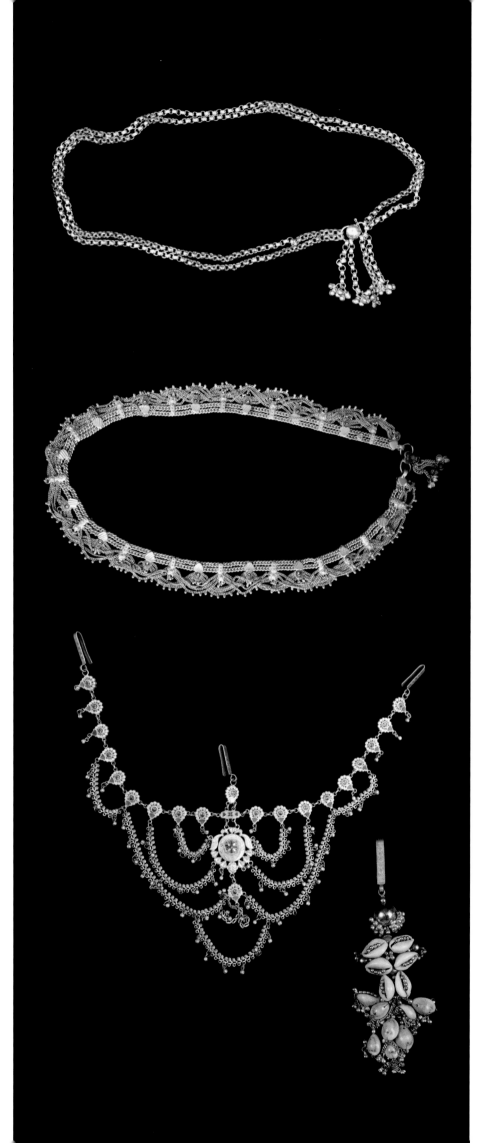

Man's *kanadoro*, waist thread,
with cotton thread tassels,
photographed in Dhar, 2014.

LEFT, FROM TOP
Man's *kanadoro* with *cheda*
(pendants) hanging from
the clasp, photographed in
Chiktiyabad tanda, 2014.

Woman's silver *kanadoro*,
photographed in Dhar, 2014.

A variation on the *kanadoro*,
this ornamental chain clips to
a woman's skirt, photographed
in Matwada tanda, 2014.

A silver and cowrie skirt clip
used to hold keys, *c.* 1980.
Maiwa collection.

OPPOSITE
Lilabai Paltiya wearing a pair
of rigid silver-wire armlets
nagmuri with a snake-like
motif and flower clasp. Note
her *kanadoro*.

Clothing and Ornament | 143

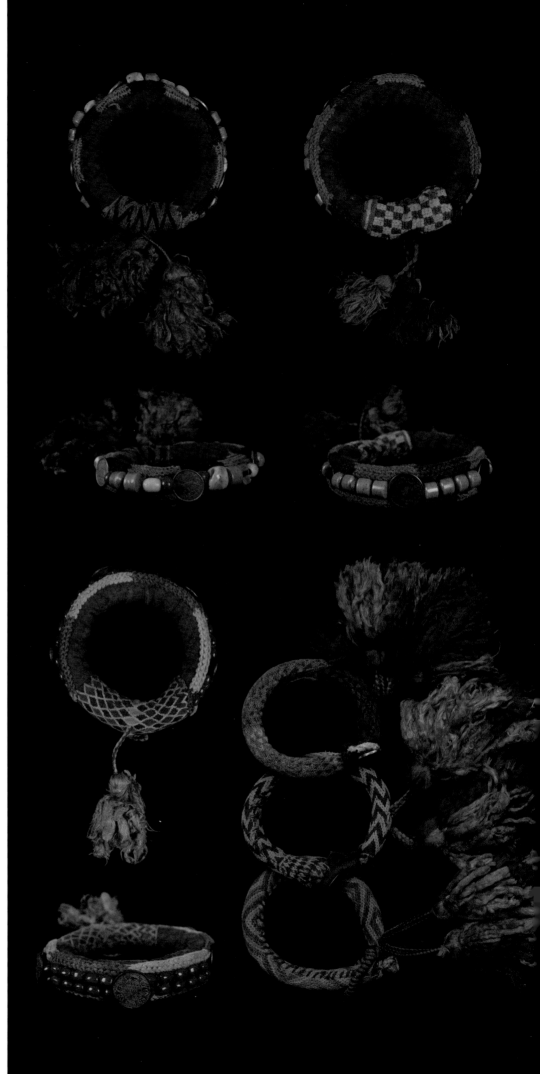

RIGHT
These cloth *pachela* are worn above the elbow and keep the bangles from striking the funny bone, *c.* 1950. Maiwa collection, except for the bottom right example which is John Childs collection.

BELOW
Armlet of hollow lead balls, each containing a metal seed. These armlets produce a faint tinkling sound whenever the wearer moves her arms, *c.* 1910. Maiwa collection.

ABOVE LEFT
A *pachela* featuring cowrie florets, lead beads, coins and an embroidered cloth band.

ABOVE RIGHT
Solid silver anklets. Each one weighs 400g.

LEFT
Hollow silver anklet. Despite being hollow, this article of jewelry weighs 300g.

BELOW LEFT
Two *pachela* made from block-printed cloth, lead beads, bells and cowries, *c.* 1940. Maiwa collection.

BELOW LEFT TO RIGHT
Double anklets. Two sets of hinged brass anklets worn in Telangana near Devarakonda, the heavy anklets are supported by a cloth anklet adorned with plastic and lead beads. Note the bells on the toe ring, 2014.

Hollow silver anklets above a much lighter silver anklet.

Cast-brass anklet or *wankidi*. This form has persisted for centuries and shows up in the 1830 painting on page 105. It is related to a similar V-shaped armlet called *vanki*. This ornament, far from being oppressive, is thought comfortable. The anklet rises at the front to a projection *gundu*, which possibly protects the foot from thorny briars when in the fields. It is crowned with a series of applied ball ornaments *cheyu*. Above it are two hinged brass anklets. Photographed near Devarakonda, Telangana, 2005.

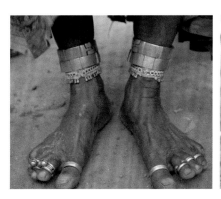

BANGLES

ABOVE
Ivory trade in East Africa
during the 1880s.

BELOW LEFT
Plastic bangles on sale in
the streets of Devarakonda,
Telangana, 2014.

BELOW RIGHT
In areas of Banjara settlement
it is possible to purchase all
the elements for traditional
embroidery: cowries, mirrors,
threads, beads, etc. It is
also possible to purchase
a pre-made synthetic
Banjara *kachali*.

Early accounts mention with wonder the number of ivory bangles worn by Banjara women. In 1794, Moore commented: 'Their arms, indeed, are so encased with ivory that it would be no easy matter to clean them.' The fashion for ivory bangles was widespread throughout rural Gujarat and Rajasthan and they were part of the traditional costume of Meghwar, Jat, Rabari and others. The tusks from Indian elephants provided a ready supply of ivory as the animal was domesticated for labour, transport and military use. The tusks of African elephants, however, were preferred as the tusks were larger and the quality of the ivory was higher. The trade from Africa to India reached its peak in the mid-nineteenth century.

> Indian products shipped to Mombassa, Mozambique, and Zanzibar were routinely exchanged for an annual average of more than two hundred tons of African ivory that entered India at Bombay and from there was distributed to all Indian craft centres. Among those are Pali in Rajasthan, Delhi, Patiala, and Hoshiarpur in Punjab, Murshidabad in West Bengal, Cuttac and Puri in Orissa. The style of work in ivory in each place is distinctive.

A full set of ivory bangles (*chudiyon*) consisted of 16 upper-arm and 12 lower-arm pieces. The bangles could be plain or grooved, drilled and inset with small gold or silver disks, dyed with lac to colour them a deep red, or bevelled and inset with bands of silver or gold around the circumference. The number of bangles in a set was determined by the craftsmen. Work was done using small handbow-driven lathes and drills. A full set of bangles for both arms would require almost a complete tusk. Those who could not afford ivory would wear bangles made from horn, coconut shell, bone or lac. Sometimes a man would give his wife one ivory bangle for each arm every year. Plastic substitutes for ivory became available in the 1950s and to this day they maintain the regional variations of the ivory they imitate. There are distinct regional styles in Telangana, Madhya Pradesh and Rajasthan. What constitutes a set is not uniform and individuals will wear as many or as few as they wish. In 1997 the jewelry historian Oppi Untracht observed that there were still about 200 craftsmen located in the traditional ivory-working centre of Pali, Rajasthan.[4] In an effort to eliminate poaching, international laws have restricted the use or sale of ivory and it is illegal to use Indian ivory in India.

These plastic bangles are made to resemble traditional ivory ones that would have been bevelled and inset with stamped gold or silver. This group referred to itself as 'Rajput Banjara'. The woman is wearing a sheer veil. When asked why they veil their faces (an uncommon gesture among the Banjara), they replied, 'That's the Rajput part.' Photographed near Jaipur, 2014.

ABOVE

A Rabari woman on migration passing through Maheshwar, Madhya Pradesh, 2014. The Rabari share similarities in ornamentation with the Banjara. This woman has added mirrors to her synthetic polka dot *choli*. She is wearing the bell-like *topli* at her temple. At her elbow is a *pachela* with bead pendants and visible through her sheer veil is a *kanadoro*. She has 22 plastic bangles on each arm, some plain, some grooved.

LEFT

Banjara still wear a complement of bangles that completely encase the arms. This woman is holding a *pulia* from the Maiwa collection, which was shown to gauge enthusiasm for reviving embroidery, Telangana, 2005.

TATTOOS

Tattoos, like clothing, express personal style, tribal identity and family connections. The dot on the left side of the nose is common to Banjara throughout most of India. Even though they are often worn willingly, such markers are perhaps best understood as the tribe marking the individual, rather than the individual choosing to show that they are a member of the tribe. In more remote areas, when Banjara encounter Westerners without tattoos, they are often puzzled: 'But how will God recognize you when you die?' they ask.

A child can be given their first tattoo when they are eight years old. Others may be added at puberty, marriage, or to avoid illness and misfortune. Like mirrors, tattoos are both decorative and protective. Decorative tattoos can be a number of auspicious designs. Women will often have the name of a close male relative tattooed on their forearm. A pattern of five dots on the chin or temple is also common. Interestingly, aside from this quincunx pattern, the repertoire of tattoo imagery is distinct from embroidery imagery. Tattoos often feature elements similar to those found in Kachchh embroidery, once gain indicating that the Banjara have their origins in north-western India.

ABOVE
Neelabai showing her forearm tattoos. The design on her upper left arm is reproduced above as a line drawing, Madakaripura tanda, Karnataka, 2014.

RIGHT
Tattoos on the back of the calf show a motif known as the 'tree of life' or 'mango tree', Malavagoppa tanda, Karnataka, 2014.

BELOW
A similar motif to that on the right is found in the embroidery of the Meghwar community residing in the Kachchh Desert, 2001. Maiwa collection.

ABOVE LEFT
A woman with the quincunx tattooed on her chin and the Banjara dot on the side of her nose, Hyderabad, 2014. The five-figure motif is often found in embroidery.

ABOVE RIGHT
This figure is a popular motif south of Hyderabad and is often found combined with the circle and dots.

LEFT
Parvathibai showing her tattoos, including a *charka* prominently displayed on her right forearm. Parvathibai is an embroiderer with the Sandur Kushala Kala Kendra embroidery project and has travelled internationally to represent the Banjara community, Sandur, 2005.

The tattooing may be done by an itinerant tattoo artist or occasionally by fellow women. In the case of travelling tattoo artists, the pattern is chosen from a selection of drawings. A little oil is spread on a ceramic tile and then held over the flame of a castor-oil lamp to catch the soot. When enough lampblack has collected it is scraped off and mixed with some oil. Other ingredients may also be added such as betel-leaf juice, cow's milk, coconut milk, or human milk. The common element in all recipes is soot. The part of the body to be tattooed is washed with cold water and the pattern is drawn on the skin with a bamboo 'pen' dipped in the soot. Three or four sewing needles are tied together and used to prick the skin. Tumeric powder is rubbed into the wound to brighten the colour and dull the pain. The addition of a tattoo is an important ceremony and so it is preceded by a blessing. The tattoo artist will often sing during the process to distract the patient and focus attention on the added beauty about to be obtained.

Just as tattooing has gained popularity in the West, it had gone out of favour with Banjara living close to or in larger cities. Such clear tribal markers are felt to be a hindrance to upward mobility. It is felt that tribal tattoos invite prejudice and make it more difficult for individuals to blend in with urban society.

BAGS

The Banjara have an assortment of bags, the most elaborate of which are given at the time of marriage and play a key part in the ceremonies. For this reason, a number of bags are sometimes called 'dowry bags'. In some areas the Banjara participated in the dowry system (where the bride's family give gifts to the groom's family) while in other areas the groom's family paid the bride's family a 'bride price'. The *Khandesh Gazetteer* records that in 1880 the 'bride price' was fifty rupees and four bullocks, but it could be as high as 1,000 rupees.

Unlike other folk embroidery, Banjara work did not function as a form of insurance where it could be sold in hard times. Embroidery was an embellishment of functional and ceremonial items and the Banjara had no history of producing work for sale. The rise of an international tourist market at the beginning of the 1960s, however, meant the Banjara began to sell their embroidery (as well as engaging in fortune telling and entertainment) in major destinations such as Goa, Mumbai and Hampi.

The bags represent a number of ingenious shapes designed to take advantage of recycled textiles. Some items, such as the man's bag (opposite), are constructed from new materials and given at weddings. While other bags, such as the smaller envelope-shaped bags, could be made from the wide embroidered band of a worn-out skirt, or from the centre piece of a ceremonial cloth. The act of embroidering the fabric, especially with tight chain stitch, gave considerable strength to the cloth. Embroidered areas would far outlast those without embroidery.

ABOVE
Neem sticks are used throughout India as a natural toothbrush. Charcoal is used as toothpaste, resulting in a messy process but very white teeth. As part of the preliminary marriage ceremony, the bride takes an embroidered *dhataniya* (a bag for tooth cleaning sticks) filled with neem sticks through the village. She offers a stick and a glass of water to each adult.

RIGHT
Dhataniya worked in cross stitch and brick stitch, photographed on location in Bhrama Kundi tanda and Dhar, Madhya Pradesh, 2014.

Man's four-sided, flat bottom bag (*sharafi kothli*) given to the groom on his wedding day. Such bags are part of a gift exchange. Depending on the local tradition, they may contain a coconut, *supari* nuts, or a set of clothing for the groom, *c.* 1940. Maiwa collection.

ABOVE
Banjara bags naturally evolve out of an affection for the square. The envelope bag is easily constructed by stitching two seams closed.

ABOVE RIGHT
An embroidered bag front and back. This bag is made from a 40-cm square embroidery that results in a finished 20-cm square bag. This one has a playful curve in the centre cross, Shimoga Hills, *c.* 1950. Maiwa collection.

RIGHT AND BELOW
An envelope bag, Shimoga Hills, *c.* 1950. Maiwa collection.

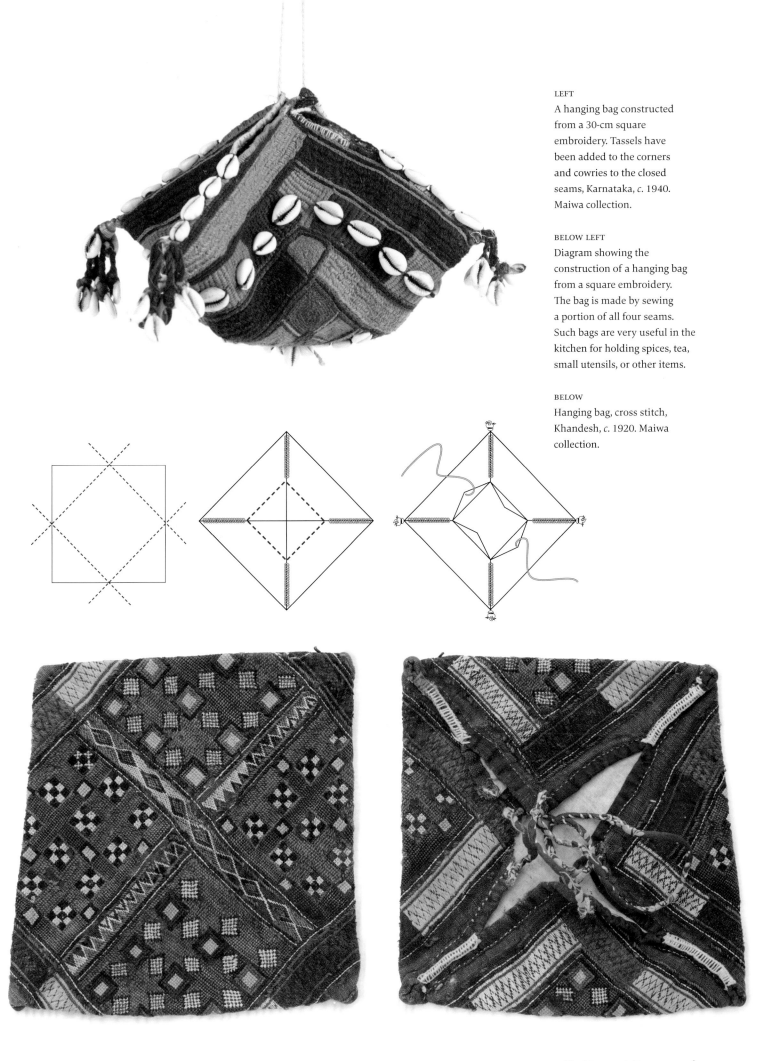

LEFT
A hanging bag constructed from a 30-cm square embroidery. Tassels have been added to the corners and cowries to the closed seams, Karnataka, *c.* 1940. Maiwa collection.

BELOW LEFT
Diagram showing the construction of a hanging bag from a square embroidery. The bag is made by sewing a portion of all four seams. Such bags are very useful in the kitchen for holding spices, tea, small utensils, or other items.

BELOW
Hanging bag, cross stitch, Khandesh, *c.* 1920. Maiwa collection.

Clothing and Ornament | 153

Two works from different collections that appear similar enough to be the work of the same hand. Because raw materials come from local markets, and works such as these are essentially made in public, they have a high degree of similarity. On the level of the stitch, however, they are quite different.

BELOW
Embroidered quilt, approx. 110 cm square. Maiwa collection.

OPPOSITE
Embroidered bag made from source cloth, 110 cm square. John Childs collection.

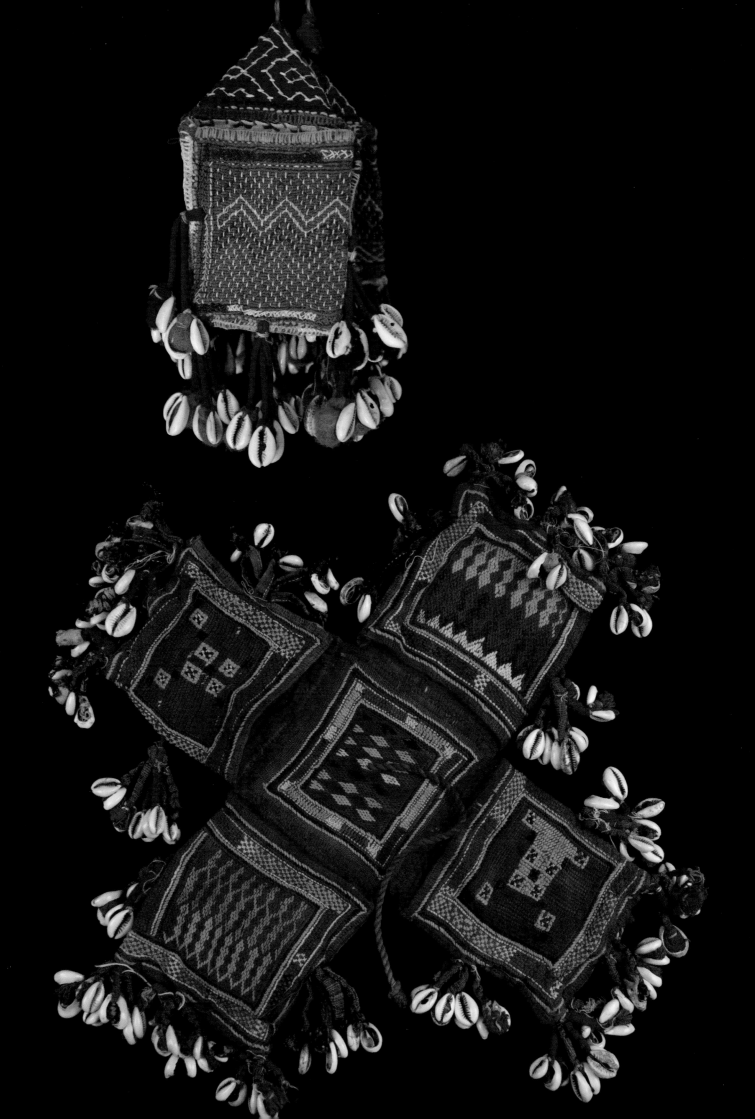

THIS PAGE
Square bags made from thick quilted fabrics adorned with cowries. Some of the bags have been stitched together to make a bag with multiple compartments. These bags range from 17 to 26 cm square, c. 1970. Maiwa collection.

OPPOSITE
Two examples of a four-sided wedding bag or *jholno*. This is a much more elaborate form of bag based on the square. Eight square pieces (four embroidered rectangles folded in half) make up the four pockets. All are sewn onto a central square that forms the top piece. A cord is attached to the centre of the top, resulting in a hanging bag. The upper bag is from the collection of John Childs, c. 1960, made from quilted fabrics. The style gives few markers as to its origin as such fabrics are found in all Banjara settlements. The date is estimated based on the attached pendants and the synthetic yarns used in the pom-poms. Below is an example of the same form worked in brick stitch from the Khandesh region with handmade indigo and madder cowrie tassels, c. 1890. Maiwa collection.

Clothing and Ornament | 157

ABOVE
These simple bags from
Karnataka are made by folding
a rectangle in half and stitching
the two seams together. Such
bags may be made new or can
be made from the salvaged
bands of old skirts, Karnataka,
c. 1940. Maiwa collection.

RIGHT
Woman's *kothli* (coin purse).
These embroidered bags
are embellished with bone
rings (bottom) and plastic
rings (right). Nora Fisher
has observed that: 'The most
significant ornaments –
ones that signal ethnicity,
lineage and community
position – are fashioned of
simple lead. In the equality
minded tanda, the wife
of the headman or naik is
only very subtly identified by
a tiny lead-adorned square
embroidered bag.' On both bags
the embroidered pouch is 7 cm
square, right: *c.* 1960, below:
c. 1910. Maiwa collection.

Three examples of a man's *supari* bag. *Supari* (*areca catechu*) or betel nut is chewed and is a mild stimulant. When sold wrapped in betel leaves, it is known as paan. These bags are 17 cm square when closed and 17 × 53 cm when open, Karnataka, *c.* 1950. Maiwa collection.

5 REVIVAL
New Masters of the Art

Embroidery has particular significance today as a language used by women to communicate their wisdom and the values they protect and nurture for themselves and for their families.

ASHOKE CHATTERJEE

The Banjara have inherited a rich folk tradition of embroidery. They are heirs to a distinctive collection of patterns and stitches that are instantly recognizable and unlike the work of any other group. The Banjara's innate design sense fits easily into a contemporary design aesthetic with its bold presentation and its notions of symmetry and play. In modern marketing parlance there is an established, well-defined brand with considerable cache. And yet to turn this cultural capital into a livelihood for skilled artisans is no simple matter. To establish a successful embroidery revival requires more than determinism, hard work and skill: it requires business savvy, an understanding of local and global markets, and the ability to motivate people to do the best work they can. And beyond all this, it requires a vision of skilled craft that can carry the distinct cultural identity of the group into the future.

In the Banjara community there have been several income-generating schemes based on needlework. Motivated by the impoverished living conditions in many Banjara tandas, social assistance programs have been implemented with the goals of relieving poverty and empowering women. Needlework, with its low start-up costs, portability, marketability and skill enhancement is the logical choice of employment for women. It provides a framework around which the goals of education, health care, family planning and so on can be built.

NGO income-generating projects, however, are often forced to maintain either the market or the craft. The NGO needs to create saleable work to make the project viable and ultimately the artisans self sufficient. However, the very nature of NGOs makes it unlikely that a market visionary will be the person directing product development. In fact, product design is frequently given to young design students from art colleges in the hope that they will tap into whatever is presently trending.

OPPOSITE

Sakuntala Reka Naik stitches a piece of embroidery on the veranda of Surya's Garden. Embroidery can be a very flexible way to augment income for women. Small pieces, threads and a needle can be carried easily and work may be fitted in around the daily routine of child care and other obligations, Kaddirampura, Karnataka, 2013.

The result is an erosion of the vital elements that make tribal embroidery distinct. It also displaces the artisan when the designer is viewed as the professional in the relationship. The results are not timeless pieces, but rather ephemeral items that reflect all too clearly the times in which they were designed. Colours are muted or 'forecast' to provide what the urban market wants. Tight or complicated stitches that make products expensive are simplified in an effort to compete with cheap goods. And, ultimately, traditional items are often considered 'old fashioned' and so these are abandoned in the hope that adding embroidered details to non-traditional items such as shirts, dresses, or saris will keep the stitch culture alive. One group even went so far as to recommend that the Banjara learn machine embroidery because it would save time and reduce costs.[1] Such advice, if followed, rapidly destroys the reputation and character of tribal embroidery. In marketing terms, it 'devalues brand equity'. In the minds of the public, Banjara embroidery is then seen as cheap, unskilled work – the type of work that can easily be copied in offshore factories.

The first embroidery projects were run by missionaries. The anecdote related at the beginning of the embroidery chapter nicely sums up the Banjara reaction to such projects: the Banjara women turn down an offer to send their children to a missionary school to learn embroidery because (in their eyes) the quality of the missionary embroidery is so poor. By retaining their independence, they retain their pride.

After partition, the government of India attempted to survey and assist in the management of the handcraft sector. In terms of embroidery, the results of this plan were realized in the 1981 Maharashtra *Handicraft Survey Report on Banjara Embroidery*. It contains excellent recommendations for establishing embroidery production, including labour and material costing, as well as the patterns needed to produce traditional items. At the time it was written, it was still possible that embroidered clothing could be produced by Banjara for the local Banjara market. That time now seems to have passed.

NGOs at work in India include the Sandur Kushala Kala Kendra (SKKK) in Karnataka. In the Sandur region many Banjara were displaced by a decade of destructive iron-ore strip mining. To get the raw ore to eastern sea ports, and ultimately China, 24-hour truck convoys (an estimated 5,000 trucks a day) took over the roads and destroyed many settlements on the route.[2] The SKKK has been a very successful project with artisans representing the Banjara community at the Santa Fe International Folk Art Market and travelling to Europe. Shantibai and Gowribai, two of their embroiderers, have won national awards. In 2010, SKKK and the Karnataka State Handicrafts Development Corporation applied for and received Geographical Indication (GI) status for the Banjara embroidery of the Sandur region.

ABOVE
Thakribai (top) and Chandrammabai working at the Sandur Kushala Kala Kendra (SKKK), 2005.

OPPOSITE
The drafted design, the printed design on fabric and finished embroidery from a Surya's Garden piece, 2014.

SURYA'S GARDEN

Surya's Garden is an embroidery initiative that grew up among the Lambani community of Hampi. A young Banjara woman, Laxmi Naik, with strong embroidery skills and hope for the future of her culture started the project in Kaddirampura with eight artisans in 2002. Naik possesses the design sense of a traditional Banjara embroiderer and the determined character of a Banjara woman. Both are necessary to manage Surya's Garden in such a way that she can revive traditional stitches, patterns and designs while still providing suitable employment for the women.

Naik is assisted in the management of Surya's Garden by her husband, Jan Duclos, a French botanist and landscape architect. Duclos has augmented Naik's textile collection of historic pieces and patterns through research into international collections. Together they work to source traditional embellishments such as the authentic black mirrors, cowries, coins and lead beads. Naik is careful to maintain the traditional palette. Her own embroidery skill sets a high benchmark for the artisans to meet.

Presently, Surya's Garden provides work for about 80 embroiderers in three tandas. The number is increasing every year. To maintain quality and orchestrate the groups, two team leaders, Laxmibai and Sumabai, work full time for the project.

There is a large Banjara population in the Hampi-Hospet area. However, many communities have lost their footing. Modern attitudes have weakened traditions as well as the historic sense of pride and independence that were central to tribal life. These values have not been replaced by education, a higher standard of living or a secure position in the modern economy. Surya's Garden works to reverse both these trends. Naik hopes that the high-quality work will give artisans a sense that the Banjara are equal to their embroidery. The project also provides a stable framework to permit women to plan for the future of their children, organize health care, stabilize family life and come together with other artisans for mutual support. Duclos is collecting a library of information on the Banjara language, Ghormati, and other aspects of their culture.

It is not easy to make contact with the market for high-quality embroidery. Moreover, such markets still need to be educated about the traditions of India's different tribal cultures and the nature of highly skilled work. But the group's desire to create collector or museum-quality work is strong. Developing the market for such high-quality work has been the role of Surya's Garden's overseas partner, Maiwa Handprints Ltd.

OPPOSITE ABOVE

A larger embroidery from Surya's Garden. Setting such pieces into appropriate products is a difficult task. An exceptional embroidery can be ruined by a sloppy tailor or by being placed on a poorly made bag. Designing products for an international market is a challenging task. Incorporating ethnographic elements into products in such a way that the aesthetic of the tribal culture is not only respected but also amplified requires dedication, skill and sensitivity, 2015. Maiwa collection.

OPPOSITE BELOW

Contemporary versions of the traditional *kalchi* (envelope bag), 2014. Maiwa collection.

BELOW

Contemporary versions of the traditional *kothli*, 2014. Maiwa collection.

LAXMI NAIK

Life, it was nice when I was small. My grandmother was a good woman and she took care of us. Both my mother and father had problems with alcohol. But my grandmother had a strong will. She fell in love with a European painter from Amsterdam who used to visit our area. The artist became my adoptive grandfather. Together they lived on an island in the Tungabhadra River a few kilometres from the Hampi temple complex. And then, when I was seventeen years old, my grandmother died.

RIGHT
Laxmi Naik, Surya's Garden, 2009.

OPPOSITE ABOVE
Poster promoting an exhibition of Banjara embroidery in Vancouver, Canada, 2012.

OPPOSITE BELOW
Embroidered *kalchi* from Surya's Garden, 2014.

I used to live in the house of my adoptive grand-father. I was working in his house when he married another woman. My life had become difficult there.

Like my grandmother, I also fell in love with a European. I married my husband, Jan Duclos, in 2002. We both knew we wanted to do something to help the Banjara community. They have a very hard life. Working in the sugar cane – a lot of drinking and many problems. I wanted very badly to try to help them. I saw what happened to my parents. They were alcoholics and did not live long.

The project started, slowly, slowly. When we first began in 2002 we had eight women. Then we expanded to 15 women. In 2005 we formed the organization into a trust. At that time we were making only cushion covers. A friend of ours in Bangalore helped us to begin to work with garments – boys' clothes, girls' clothes, shirts and dresses. We were able to go to Bangalore and sell things. Sometimes tourists came to visit us and we would sell directly to them.

In 2008 we went to Gujarat. There we met Meena Raste who worked for the Kutch Mahila Vikas Sangathan (KMVS). We saw a book called *Through the Eye of a Needle* about the embroidery of the Kachchh tribal women. And from that meeting we first heard about the Canadian woman, Charllotte Kwon, and her store, Maiwa.

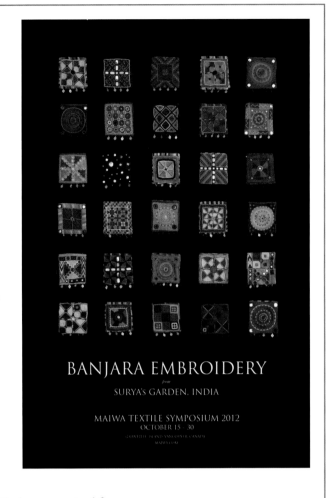

BANJARA EMBROIDERY

from

SURYA's GARDEN. INDIA

MAIWA TEXTILE SYMPOSIUM 2012
OCTOBER 15 - 30
GRANVILLE ISLAND VANCOUVER CANADA
MAIWA.COM

Many people say that there is no other embroidery project like ours. That is because my husband Jan is working very hard to find old pieces. We find them in museums and books, and we make trips to visit other Banjara communities in India. Jan takes photos of the work. From these, we lay out the patterns that guide the young embroiderers. We are very careful to make our embroideries the best. It is not easy. It is difficult to even get the right colour threads. Old ornaments: coins, cowries and mirrors are almost impossible to find.

This year we have 60 women. At the moment ten are away working to harvest sugar cane. There are so many festivals, so many other things that our embroidery must work around. We have two team leaders. Each month we have a meeting and the team leaders look at who is doing good work. Every day they work in a group. There are five or six ladies together. Our team leaders are strong enough to hold them together.

Now they start to understand that this work – it is our work. We feel strongly that we want to do this. After 20 years maybe there will be nothing left. We work to preserve what we can. What I feel is that it is important for my community. It is important for me. Because we don't have writing or reading – nothing is there. That is why we keep our worn clothing.

ABOVE

Naik and Duclos work on
creating new textiles that will
both maintain traditional styles
and stitches and be viable in
an international market. Based
on their own collection, and
time spent examining other
collections throughout the
world, they select combinations
of patterns, colours and
stitches that will work in
a variety of sizes. Duclos
drafts designs on paper.
The process is a meditative
one that he very much enjoys.

RIGHT

Duclos examines the finished
drawings for the larger
embroideries. Based on
the drawings, designs are
transferred onto cloth and
the details added. The process
takes considerable time but
gives Surya's Garden the
opportunity to create pieces
that will carry the genius
of Banjara embroidery into
the future, Kaddirampura,
Karnataka, 2013.

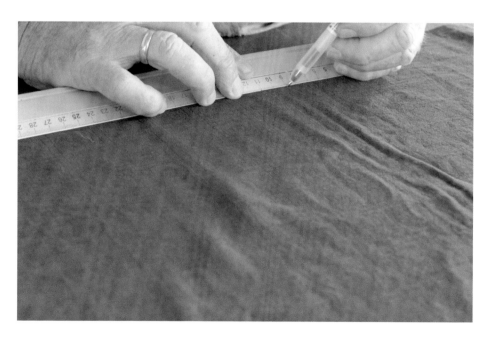

In 2001, Maiwa attended the *Embroidery: Creativity and Tradition* seminar, sponsored by the Crafts Council of India, which was held in Hyderabad. At that time, Maiwa had already been working with tribal cultures in Kachchh for a number of years and was in the process of planning a museum exhibition. At this time, the Banjara community around Hyderabad was still producing extraordinary work. Maiwa conducted a number of research trips in Andhra Pradesh and Karnataka to explore the possibility of working directly with a Banjara tanda. In 2008, Maiwa was contacted by Surya's Garden in Kaddirampura – they received a hand-written letter with flowing prose and an eloquent invitation for them to visit Surya's Garden and see the work first hand. In 2009, the two groups came together in a typically India way: what was supposed to be a six-hour drive for Charllotte Kwon and her manager Shirley Gordon turned into 23 hours negotiating potholes and wash-outs. It left only a few short hours for a meeting before it was time to make the return journey. But the seeds had been planted.

From Maiwa's perspective, Surya's Garden was perfect. Naik and Duclos were trying to create high-quality work but were having difficulty with product design, costing and connecting to a more affluent market. Maiwa's attempts to work with Banjara tandas had failed because Maiwa lacked a permanent presence close to the communities they wanted to work with. Perhaps the two groups could succeed by working together. Maiwa sent photographs of its Banjara collection and Surya's Garden expanded its designs. In 2012, Naik and her husband travelled to Vancouver with their infant son Solal. They staged an exhibition of embroidery, conducted workshops on Banjara stitches and presented a lecture on the history and culture of the Banjara.

Surya's Garden has faced considerable adversity in its struggle to survive. The project is named after Naik and Duclos's first child, who died when he was struck down by a drunken driver. But the group now has an international reputation and an expanding product line. Presently, Duclos assists Naik by drafting traditional design patterns onto *chhatya* cloth to distribute to the artisans. Women work in

The base cloth as the embroiderer sees it. The cloth is marked with the colours of threads and the stitches to be placed in each area, Kaddirampura, Karnataka, 2013.

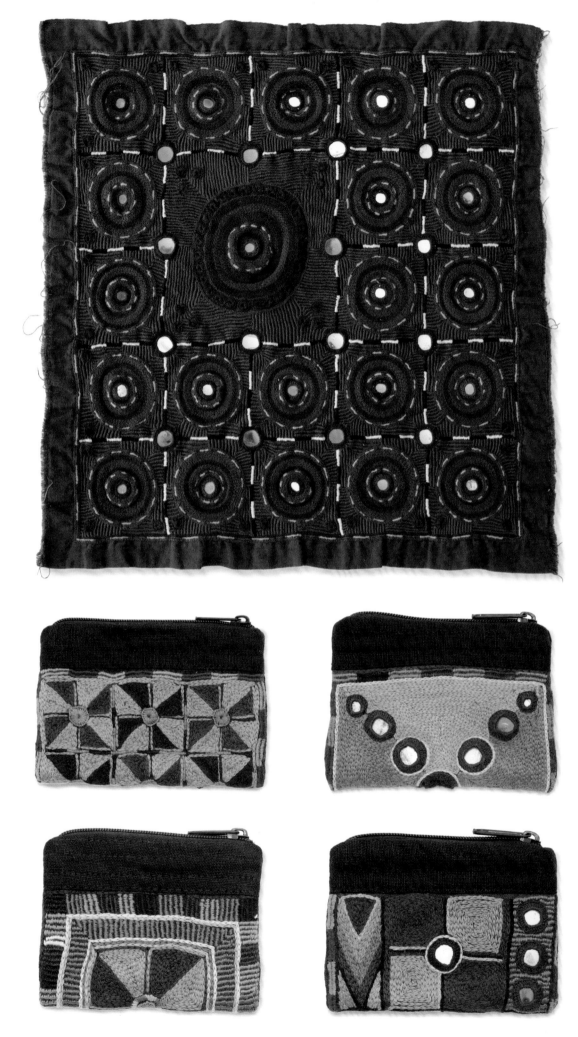

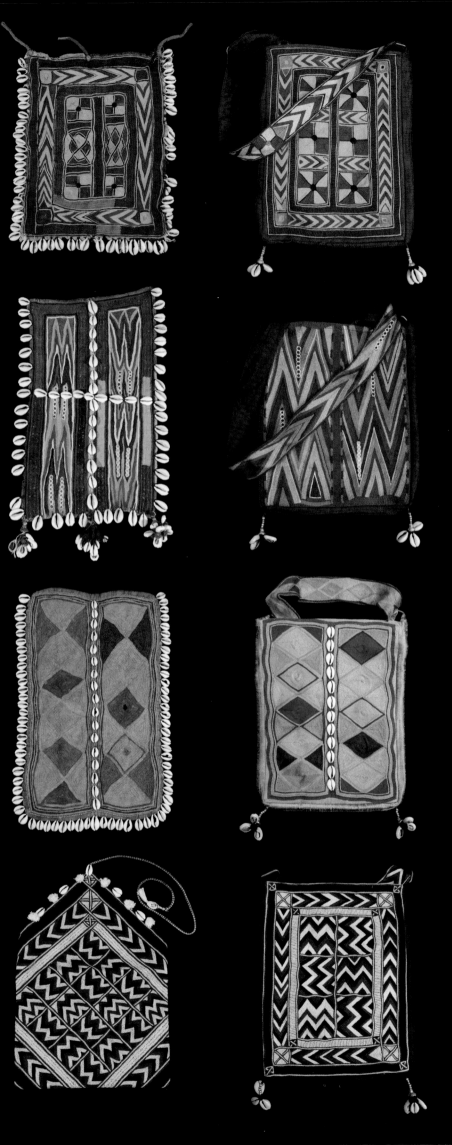

OPPOSITE ABOVE

Revival work being done by Surya's Garden. A combination of traditional stitches in an almost monochromatic framework. Such works lead back to historic pieces and motivate the curious to discover their connections.

OPPOSITE BELOW

Small pieces are essential to a revival project. They permit women to join without a prohibitive time commitment. They also allow for skill-building as small pieces may be completed and evaluated in a very short time. Women may also get paid small amounts quickly, allowing them greater financial independence.

LEFT

Four new bags (right) and their historic inspiration (left). Banjara embroidery displays a highly creative play with pattern, colour and motif. Often a very subtle resetting of traditional work is all that is necessary in order to create contemporary pieces.

New Masters of the Art | 171

TOP
(left to right) Charllotte Kwon,
Meena Raste and Laxmibai
meet with Piklibai (seated),
Maramanahalli tanda,
Karnataka, 2013.

ABOVE
Laxmibai (a team leader for
Surya's Garden) works a chain
stitch in blue thread, Surya's
Garden, Kaddirampura,
Karnataka, 2014.

ABOVE RIGHT
Laxmibai (in blue) meets
Meena Raste and Charllotte
Kwon to talk about stitches,
Surya's Garden, 2011.

their homes and some bring their children with them when they embroider at Surya's Garden. Duclos has planted rare and beautiful species of plants throughout the grounds. Naik's hope is that one day the women will be skilled enough to take over some of the design and pattern creation themselves. The ultimate goal is for the artisans to claim their stitch heritage as if it was never lost. The connection is more delicate than most people imagine. It only takes one generation of neglect to lose the skills that a group has carried for centuries. The pattern sense and embroidery knowledge used to be passed from mother to daughter as part of family life. Embroidery was done for an hour or two every day and children learned stitches as they would learn to speak: unconsciously, without realizing what they were learning.

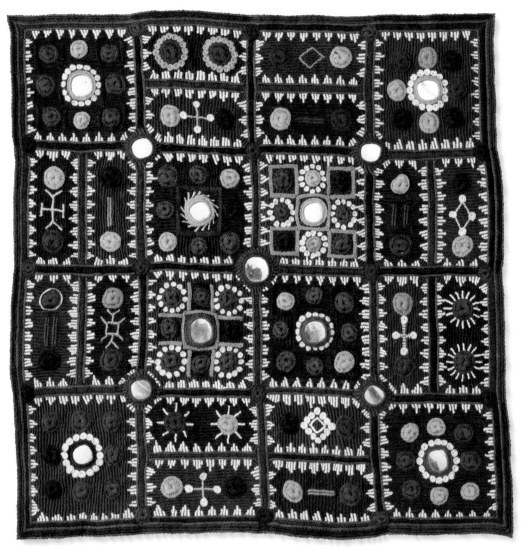

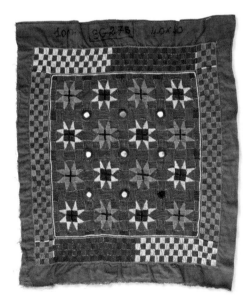

Now learning is passed from elder to apprentice as part of a craft trust. If the work is done in a domestic setting, the next generation naturally picks up embroidery skills. Today, prestige for the women is gained from being the primary wage-earners in the family. Embroidery is no longer seen as a marker of backwardness but as something that requires skill and knowledge to create. The fact that embroidery is so highly regarded outside the community reintroduces its value in

THIS PAGE
Embroiderers spend the
morning dressing in full
traditional Banjara costume.
Shila Chandra, above right,
was pregnant on the day of
the photo shoot. She gave
birth to a boy that evening,
Surya's Garden, Kaddirampura,
Karnataka, 2013.

OPPOSITE ABOVE, LEFT TO RIGHT
Devi Chandra, Sarda Ravi,
Sakuntala Reka, Laxmibai
Gopi, Sunita Vithoba, Laxmi,
Laxmibai Pomiya, Sumabai
Tipa, Mina Sina, Shakuntla
Krishna, Shila Chandra,
Sakuntala Sina (they all
share the surname Naik).

OPPOSITE BELOW
Embroiderers in full traditional
Banjara costume, Surya's
Garden, Kaddirampura,
Karnataka, 2013.

a modern setting, suggesting that it need not be discarded as the culture imagines
itself in the future.

Some of the older women still dress in traditional style but most of the younger
generation are not familiar with the Banjara costume. Naik herself prefers modern
clothing and is astonished at how heavy the entire ensemble of dress and ornament
can be. In 2013, a group of the younger embroiderers agreed to dress traditionally
for a photo shoot in the Garden. There was much laughter as the courtyard filled
with women who had never before worn the traditional clothing of their culture.

CONCLUSION

It is often said that embroidery is a language: a semiotic system for communicating through colour, pattern, stitch and embellishment. It follows a grammar that orders elements and prohibits inappropriate combinations. If embroidery is a language and the tradition is well established, it may also give rise to dialects: minor flourishes that are regionally distinct. To take the linguistic analogy further, most of the markers that permit an opinion to be formed about a person speaking do not depend on the words spoken. Accent, tone and pronunciation all provide clues to the personality, class, background, education and regional history of a speaker. This is the role of embroidery also, to express the identity of the maker in terms of family, community, skill, heritage, creativity and tradition. If the loss of embroidery is tragic, it is tragic for exactly this reason: it is the disappearance of the expressions of individuals worked within the framework of their culture. Contained within the threads put down on cloth is a way of seeing the world and interpreting its rules. The culture forms the rules and the individual follows, bends, or breaks them, thus redefining the culture for the next generation. Embroidery brings beauty into the world from almost nothing (a few threads, some cloth and a needle), and its loss is the disappearance of a way of bringing beauty and meaning into existence.

Appendix: Line Drawings

The density of Banjara stitchwork often overshadows the architecture of the patterns. These line drawings are included to give an alternative representation of some key pieces. The works shown here are all embroidered with stitches that fully cover the ground fabric.

With two exceptions, these line drawings illustrate the highly visible *pulia* worn behind the head when carrying water. Figure **a** is a ceremonial cloth and figure **g** is a *garna*. For an explanation of the use of these textiles see page 133.

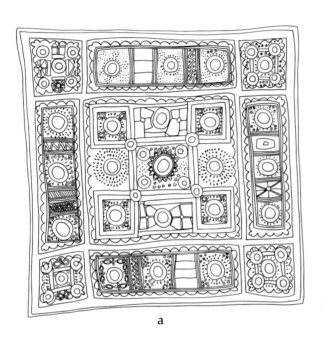

a

b

c

d

e

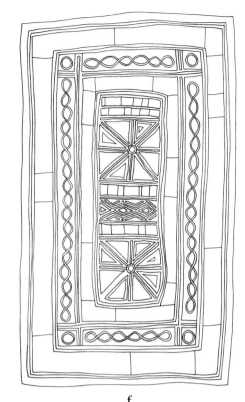

f

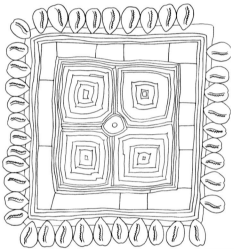

g

h

i

Acknowledgments

We came to this subject not as trained anthropologists, curators or historians, but as two people with an interest in the culture of textiles. As a result, our hope was not so much to declare the objective truth of one of the most fascinating cultures in India, so much as to suggest the contours of their story and to show the forceful beauty of the people and their work.

The more we studied the Banjara, the more we understood that vast portions of who they are would not fit into this book. A look at their religion could fill many volumes, as would a look at the sub-groups, their genealogies, creation stories, songs and folktales.

We have been generous in quoting those who have met the Banjara so that the character of the observer will come through. As far as possible, we have endeavoured to track all quotations back to their original sources. We have left out much that we feel is suspicious or unsubstantiated in the colonial ethnographies. If there are errors of omission, inclusion or interpretation, we are entirely culpable.

This work grew out of embroidery research that began in the mid-1990s and has focused on the Banjara specifically since 2001. Together we are indebted to John Gillow for his introduction to Thames & Hudson, his generous friendship and seemingly limitless knowledge of textiles. At Thames & Hudson we would like to extend our appreciation to our editors, Jamie Camplin and Julian Honer, and to the talented editorial and design team who so skilfully managed this project. Among the Banjara, Laxmi Naik has led us well and maintained a clear hope for the future of her tribe. Together with her husband Jan Duclos, the two have taken great risks, succeeded and created some of the finest embroidery being stitched anywhere in the world.

Our travels in India are facilitated to no small extent by the quick thinking of Mahesh Dosaya, who we are proud to have known long enough to call family. Meena Raste was always several steps ahead of us. On the few occasions that we thought we had lost her she was already in the village surrounded by a group of women talking embroidery. Few can match her knowledge of stitchwork or tribal cultures. Her husband Pankaj Shah is an expert collector of information, a quick wit and a gifted facilitator when organizing embroidery projects.

On our 2014 trip we enlisted the capable help of Ravinder Padya to assist with translation and introductions to Banjara groups in Telangana and Madhya Pradesh. He not only understood our project immediately, but was also able to communicate our goals quickly to others. We threw him into some tricky situations and he acquitted himself admirably.

In Madhya Pradesh, Sally Holkar was an enthusiastic partner in tracking down leads to the Banjara community. She tempered our long days with friendship and thoughtfulness and our time with her has inspired future projects. Bhangya Bhukya arranged a number of connections for us and freely gave of his valuable time at Osmania University. In Karnataka, Laxmi Naik and Jan Duclos made many of the initial contacts with tandas. There we were assisted in translation and introductions by Balu Rathod, Shiva Maygeri and Dr Mannur. In Maheshwar, Prakash Pawar guided us to many tandas and opened the doors to his community.

We would like to thank Rosemary Crill of the Victoria and Albert Museum for arranging access to the collection and for graciously agreeing to contribute the foreword for this book. The staff of numerous libraries have been invaluable but those of the British Library in London deserve special mention, as does the institution itself.

The Maiwa Foundation has been generous in supporting Banjara embroidery projects as well as several initial attempts to track down the embroiderers. The foundation purchased many key textiles from an initial interest, not knowing that such works would shortly be unavailable. Without the foundation, or those who have contributed to it, there would be little revival to document. To the company, Maiwa Handprints Ltd, we are grateful that this book was believed to be not only possible, but necessary. Maiwa is not a university, but they have acted like one in supporting the considerable time needed to prepare this manuscript, and in providing the space and research resources necessary to grasp such an extensive and far-reaching subject fully. Over many years, Elizabeth Yoon has encouraged us with her firm belief in the potential of craft – she has been a key supporter and an unfailing friend.

In Vancouver, we have benefited from the extensive stitch knowledge of Toby Smith and Bonnie Adie. Late in our research, John Childs contacted us after visiting the Maiwa store in Vancouver and told us that he had a few pieces that we might find interesting. We spent the entire afternoon at his home in the UK, examining and photographing what is perhaps one of the best collections of Banjara work we have ever seen. Our gratitude to him is indeed deep.

We owe a debt beyond measuring to the openness of the Banjara community. We walked into their tandas as strangers and they welcomed us, brought out their heirlooms and answered our questions. On many occasions, they permitted us to set up a makeshift studio to photograph their embroidery, clothing, jewelry and themselves. It is our hope that this book will repay their confidence and friendship through presenting to the world some small portion of their history and preserving the enduring legacy of their work.

Pole Palli tanda, Telangana, 2014

Photo Credits

With the exception of the images mentioned below, all photographs were taken by Tim McLaughlin between 2005 and 2015. Other credits are:

Charllotte Kwon: pages 23, 33, 35 (bottom), 58, 60, 124, 145 (bottom left) and 163.

Eiluned Edwards: inset images of mirror-makers, page 105.

Gaja Digital Agency: pages 162, 172 (inset).

K. L. Kamat (kamat.com): page 80.

Line drawings in the appendix are by Sophena Kwon.

Notes

A STRONG THREAD
**The Banjara and their
Embroidery pp. 12–19**

1 N. Fisher, 'Banjara: Adornment of a People of All India' in *Mud, Mirror and Thread*, 1993, 144.

2 The language is also known as Ghormati, Banjari and Lamani. C. H. Childers, 'Banjaras' in L. S. Leshnik and G. Sontheimer (eds), *Pastoralists and Nomads in South Asia*, 1975, 247. Ability to speak Ghorboli is also used by the All India Banjara Seva Sangh. R. Naik, *Report of the All India Banjara Study Team*, All India Banjara Seva Sangh (AIBSS), 1968.

HISTORY
Empire of the Caravan pp. 20–89

1 E. Kitts, *Report on the Census of Berar*, 1881, 150.

2 E. Balfour, *The Cyclopaedia of India*, 1885, 3rd edn, v1, 270.

3 Childers, *op. cit.*, 247–48.

4 N. B. Tomašević and R. Djurić, *Gypsies of the World*, 1989, 17. Also D. Kenrick, *Gypsies: from the Ganges to the Thames*, 2004, 4.

5 Field research, 2014. Interview with geneologist and oral historian Ramjol Naik Lavudia. Prithviraj Chauhan was in conflict with Mahmood Ghori (1162–1206) who ended the Ghaznivid reign. Mahmood Ghori's successor founded the Delhi Sultanate.

6 I. Hancock, 'The Emergence of Romani as a Koïné Outside of India' in *Scholarship and the Gypsy Struggle: Commitment in Romani Studies*, 2000, 1.

7 N. Rai, G. Chaubey, R. Tamang, et al., 'The Phyylogeography of Y-Chromosome Haplogroup H1a1a-M82 Reveals the Likely Indian Origin of the European Romani Populations', 2012 in PLoS ONE, 7(11).

8 I. Habib, 'Merchant communities in precolonial India' in J. D. Tracy (ed.), *The Rise of Merchant Empires*, 1993, 373–74.

9 S. Wolpert, *A New History of India*, 7th edn, 2004, 115.

10 'Udaipur State' in *Imperial Gazetteer of India*, 1909, v24, 202.

11 J. Briggs, 'Account of the Origin, History, and Manners of the Race of Men Called Bunjaras' in *Transactions of the Literary Society of Bombay*, 1819, 172.

12 W. Francis, *Madras District Gazetteers: Vizagapatam*, 1907, 264.

13 Habib, *op. cit.*, 373.

14 *Ibid.*, 374.

15 Briggs, *op. cit.*, 196.

16 *Gazetteer of the Province of Oudh*, 1877, v1, 123.

17 T. Roe in W. Foster (ed.), *The Embassy of Sir Thomas Roe to India 1615–19*, 1926, 67.

18 P. Mundy in R. C. Temple (ed.), *The Travels of Peter Mundy*, 1914, 95.

19 *Ibid.*, 95–96.

20 *Ibid.*, 96.

21 M. Alam and S. Subrahmanyam, *Indo-Persian Travels*, 2007, 352.

22 J.-B. Tavernier in W. Crooke (ed.), *Travels in India*, 1925, 33.

23 Kitts, *op. cit.*, 150.

24 Tavernier, *op. cit.*, 42.

25 J. Albrecht de Mandelslo, 'Voyages and Travels' in J. Harris (ed.), *Navigantium atque Itinerantium Bibliotheca*, 1666, 130.

26 Habib, *op. cit.*, p. 376.

27 Wolpert, *op. cit.*, 168.

28 W. Hansen, *The Peacock Throne*, 1972, 485.

29 R. Orme, *A History of the Military Transactions of the British Nation*, 1973, v2, 102.

30 *Ibid.*

31 J. Goldworth Alger 'James Forbes' in *Dictionary of National Biography*, 1749–1819, v19.

32 James Forbes, *Oriental Memoirs*, 1813, v3, 254–55.

33 *Ibid.*

34 *Ibid.*

35 T. Seccombe 'Edward Moore' in *Dictionary of National Biography*, 1885–1900, v38.

36 E. Moor, *A Narrative of the Operations*, 1794, 131–32.

37 *Ibid.*

38 *Ibid.*

39 *Ibid.*

40 *Ibid.*

41 M. Wilks, *Historical Sketches*, 1817, 208–209.

42 *Ibid.*

43 Briggs, *op. cit.*, 186.

44 *Ibid.*

45 'Measures adopted for obtaining the assistance of the Banjaras', IOR/F/4/59/1313.

46 *Ibid.*

47 E. Bell, *Memoir of General John Briggs*, 1885, 40.

48 J. Kenneth Severn, *Architects of Empire*, 2007, 121.

49 A. Wellesley in J. Gurwood (ed.), *The Dispatches*, 1837, v1, 217.

50 Briggs, *op. cit.*, 187.

51 *Ibid.*, 189.

52 *Ibid.*

53 Wellesley, *op. cit.*, 597.

54 Briggs, *op. cit.*, 185.

55 Wellesley, *op. cit.*, 631.

56 *Ibid.*, 597–98.

57 *Ibid.*

58 Richard Holmes, *Wellington: The Iron Duke*, 2002, 62.

59 Wellesley, *op. cit.*, 598.

60 Wolpert, *op. cit.*, 200.

61 J. Keay, *India*, 361.

62 Wolpert, *op. cit.*, 204.

63 'Criminal Tribes Act' in J. Marriott and B. Mukhopadhyay (eds), *Britain in India, 1765–1905*, 228–39.

64 Francis Buchanan, *A Journey from Madras*, 1807, v2, 174.
65 *Ibid.*, 182.
66 J. Dubois, *Hindu Manners, Customs, and Ceremonies*, 1817, 68.
67 *Ibid.*, 70.
68 N. Dirks, *Castes of Mind*, 2003, 21.
69 Dubois, *op. cit.* (1906 edn), viv.
70 *Ibid.*, xv.
71 J. Mill, *History of British India*, 1817, v1, xv.
72 N. F. Cumberlege, 'Sketch of the Banjáras of Berár' in A. C. Lyall (ed.), *Gazetteer for the Haidárabád Assigned Districts*, 1870, 195.
73 *Ibid.*, 196.
74 Balfour, *op. cit.*, 272.
75 Briggs, *op. cit.*, 178.
76 *Ibid.*, 182.
77 J. Tod, *Annals and Antiquities of Rajasthan*, 1829, 570.
78 *Ibid.*, 571.
79 V. Ball, *Jungle Life in India*, 1880, 516.
80 *Ibid.*, 517.
81 Keay, *op. cit.*, 407.
82 J. Malcolm, *A Memoir of Central India*, 1823, v2, 92.
83 *Ibid.*, 96.
84 *Ibid.*, 201.
85 *Ibid.*, 152.
86 Tod, *op. cit.*, 570.
87 *Ibid.*, 572–73.
88 *Ibid.*
89 Tod, *op. cit.*, 571.
90 E. Balfour, 'On the Migratory Tribes of Natives in Central India', reprinted in *Journal of the Asiatic Society*, 1844, 3.
91 *Ibid.*, 4.
92 Balfour, *Cyclopaedia*, 271.
93 *Ibid.*
94 T. Macaulay, 'Minute on Education' in *Selections from Educational Records: 1781–1839*, 1965.
95 D. A. Washbrook, 'Progress and Problems' in P. O'Brian (ed.), *Industrialization: Critical Perspectives on the World Economy*, v4, 257.

96 C. A. Bayly, *Rulers, Townsmen and Bazaars*, 2014, 269.
97 Washbrook, *op. cit.*, 246.
98 J. Strachey and R. Strachey, *The Finances and Public Works of India*, 1882, 219.
99 B. Bhukya, *Subjugated Nomads*, 2010, 74.
100 *Ibid.*, 87.
101 Briggs, *op. cit.*, 174.
102 *Indian Railway History*, http://www.irfca.org/faq/faq-hist.html, accessed 16 September 2014.
103 H. MacKenzie, *Report of the Revised Settlement of the Goojerat District, in the Rawul Pindee Division*, 1861, 37.
104 D. Ibbetson, *Punjab Castes*, 1916, 255.
105 J. M. Campbell, *Gazetteer of the Bombay Presidency: Khandesh*, 1880, 108.
106 Bhukya, *op. cit.*, 103.
107 Briggs, *op. cit.*, 191.
108 Dirks, *op. cit.*, 129.
109 L. Leigh, 'Vagrancy and the Criminal Law' in T. Cook (ed.), *Vagrancy: Some New Perspectives*, 1979, 95.
110 Maria Yellow Horse Brave Heart, http://www.historicaltrauma.com/, accessed 16 September 2014.
111 *Criminal Tribes Act*, 1871.
112 E. J. Gunthorpe, *Notes on the Criminal Tribes*, 1882, unpaginated preface.
113 *Ibid.*, 43.
114 F. S. Mullaly, *Notes on the Criminal Classes of the Madras Presidency*, 1892, 31.
115 J. Falconer (ed.), *The Waterhouse Albums: Central Indian Provinces*, 2009, 149.
116 J. F. Watson and J. W. Kaye (eds), *The People of India*, v7, plate, 366.
117 Dirks, *op. cit.*, 181.
118 *Ibid.*, 183.
119 *Ibid.*, 184.
120 *Ibid.*, 185.
121 E. Thurston, *Castes and Tribes of Southern India*, v4, 231.

122 M. Parr and G. Badger, *The Photobook: A History*, 2004, v1, 47.
123 J. Falconer 'A Passion for Documentation' in V. Dehejia and C. Allen (eds), *India Through the Lens*, 2000, 82.
124 Childers, *op. cit.*, 251.
125 *Ibid.*, 255.
126 W. Crooke, *The Tribes and Castes of the North-Western Provinces and Oudh*, 1896, v1, 164.
127 D. B. Naik, *The Art and Literature of Banjara Lambanis*, 2000, 1.
128 R. G. Varady, 'North Indian Banjaras: Their Evolution as Transporters' in *South Asia: Journal of South Asian Studies*, 1979, 2: 1–2, 11.
129 Cumberlege, *op. cit.*, 195.
130 The Indian Act (Canada), signed 19 April 1884.
131 Bhukya, *op. cit.*, 227.

EMBROIDERY
Song of the Cloth pp. 90–109
1 Fisher, *op. cit.*, 155.
2 D. Bhagvat and P. Jayakar, 'Embroidery in India' in R. G. Billington (ed.), *Review 1972/3 CIBA GEIGY*, 1973, 9
3 J. Graham, 'Ladders of Life. Review of Exhibitions "Banjara" and "Gotter Tiere, Blumen"' in *Hali*, no. 39, 1988.
4 To specify the time and circumstances under which 'pre-Mughal' becomes 'Mughal' (roughly 1630), Graham defers to Robin Skelton's study of the use of Mughal motifs: 'A Decorative Motif in Mughal Art' in P. Pal (ed.), *Aspects of Indian Art*, 1972, 148.
5 B. Dupaigne and F. Cousin, *Afghan Embroidery*, 1996, 82.
6 Thurston, *op. cit.*, v4, 215.
7 Tavernier, *op. cit.*, 28.
8 Fisher, *op. cit.*, 152.

BANJARA STYLE
Clothing and Ornament
pp. 110–159
1 'Handicraft Survey Report: Banjara Embroidery' in K. V. Ramswami (ed.), *Census of India: Maharashtra*, 1981 and 1988, 41.
2 *Ibid.*, 37.
3 J. Frater, *Threads of Identity*, 1995, 103.
4 O. Untracht, *Traditional Jewelry of India*, 1997, 177.

REVIVAL
New Masters of the Art
pp. 160–177
1 From *Banjara Embroidery* (recommendations from the Crafts Council of Andhra Pradesh to the Banjara Needlecraft Project in Yallamma Tanda, unpaginated)
'One of the major problems faced by the Banjaran ladies is that the articles made are too colourful and loud for the urban taste. We suggested that they use pastel shades as well instead of the traditional red, blue, black and green....
Moreover the lightly embroidered pieces would reduce the cost price of the articles and thus would enable higher sales. We explained the benefits that they would get if they made lightly embroidered pieces – less time required, more articles can be made in the same time, more sales, higher income.
We encouraged them to use different types of stitches rather than just to stick to the mirror work. Again the threads that are used are only cotton and they were unwilling to try out silk or zari threads for embroidery. We also suggested that they should learn to embroider using machines as it would save time, be less tedious and also lower their costs. But they refused to try it.'
2 Field work, 2005, 2006.

Bibliography

Alam, Muzaffar and Sanjay Subrahmanyam, *Indo-Persian Travels in the Age of Discoveries 1400–1800* (Cambridge, 2007).

Alger, John Goldworth, 'James Forbes', *Dictionary of National Biography*, 1749–1819.

Balfour, Edward, *The Cyclopaedia of India and of Eastern and Southern Asia, Commercial, Industrial, and Scientific; Products of the Mineral, Vegetable, and Animal Kingdoms, Useful Arts and Manufactures* (3rd edn, London, 1885).

— 'On the Migratory Tribes of Natives in Central India' reprinted in *Journal of the Asiatic Society* (Bengal, 1844).

Ball, Valentine, *Jungle Life in India; or the Journeys and Journals of an Indian Geologist* (London, 1880).

Barnden, Betty, *The Embroidery Stitch Bible* (Iola, 2003).

Bates, Crispin, 'Race, Caste and Tribe in Central India: The Early Origins of Indian Anthropometry' in Peter Robb (ed.), *The Concept of Race in South Asia* (New Delhi, 2011).

Bayly, C. A., *Rulers, Townsmen and Bazaars: North Indian Society in the Age of British Expansion* (New Delhi, 2014).

Bell, Evans, *Memoir of General John Briggs of the Madras Army with Comments on Some of his Words and Works* (London, 1885).

Beste, Michael, *Die Banjara und ihre Stickereien* (Abenden, 2002).

Benett, William Charles (ed.), *Gazetteer of the Province of Oudh* (Lucknow, 1877).

Bhagvat, Durga, and Pramila

Jayakar, 'Embroidery in India' in R. G. Billington (ed.), *Review 1972/3 CIBA GEIGY* (Basel, 1973).

Bhukya, Bhangya, *Subjugated Nomads: The Lambadas under the Rule of the Nizams* (Hyderabad, 2010).

Briggs, John, 'Account of the Origin, History, and Manners of the Race of Men Called Bunjaras' in *Transactions of the Literary Society of Bombay* (Bombay, 1819).

Buchanan, Francis, *A Journey from Madras through the Countries of Mysore, Canara, and Malabar* (London, 1807).

Burman, J. J. Roy, *Ethnography of a Denotified Tribe* (New Delhi, 2010).

Campbell, James M., *Gazetteer of the Bombay Presidency: Khandesh* (Bombay, 1880).

Childers, C. H., 'Banjaras' in L. S. Leshnik and G. Sontheimer (eds), *Pastoralists and Nomads in South Asia* (Wiesbaden, 1975).

Crill, Rosemary, *Indian Embroidery* (London, 1999).

Crooke, William, *The Tribes and Castes of the North-Western Provinces and Oudh* (Calcutta, 1896).

— *The Head-dress of Banjara Women* (Patna, 1918).

Cumberlege, N. F., 'Sketch of the Banjáras of Berár' in A. C. Lyall (ed.), *Gazetteer for the Haidárabád Assigned Districts* (Bombay, 1870).

Deogaonkar, S. G., and Shailaja S. Deogaonkar, *The Banjara* (New Delhi, 1992).

Dirks, Nicholas, *Castes of Mind: Colonialism and the Making of Modern India* (Princeton, 2013).

Dubois, Jean-Antoine in Henry Beauchamp (ed.), *Hindu Manners, Customs, and Ceremonies* (Oxford, 1906).

Dupaigne, Bernard, and Francoise Cousin, *Afghan Embroidery* (Karachi, 1996).

Elliot, Henry M., *Memoirs of the History, Folk-lore, and Distribution of the Races of the North Western Provinces of India* (2nd edn, London, 1869).

Enthoven, Reginald Edward, *The Tribes and Castes of Bombay* (Bombay, 1922).

Falconer, John, 'A Passion for Documentation' in Vidya Dehejia and Charles Allen (eds), *India Through the Lens* (Washington, 2000).

— (ed.), *The Waterhouse Albums: Central Indian Provinces* (London, 2009).

Fisher, Nora, 'Banjara: Adornment of a People of All India' in *Mud, Mirror and Thread* (Ahmedabad, 1993).

Forbes, James, *Oriental Memoirs: a Narrative of Seventeen Years Residence in India* (2nd edn, London, 1834).

Francis, W., *Madras District Gazetteers: Vizagapatam* (Madras, 1907).

Frater, Judy, *Threads of Identity: Embroidery and Adornment of the Nomadic Rabaris* (Ahmedabad, 1995).

Furse, George Armand, *Military Transport* (London, 1882).

Gillow, John, and Nicholas Barnard, *Traditional Indian Textiles* (London, 1993).

Graham, Joss, 'Ladders of Life. Review of Exhibitions "Banjara" and "Gotter Tiere, Blumen"' in *Hali*, no. 39 (London, 1988).

— 'Banjara Embroidery' in *Embroidery*, 43 (3) (Surrey, 1992).

Gunthorpe, E. J., *Notes on Criminal Tribes Residing in or Frequenting The Bombay Presidency, Berar and The Central Provinces* (Bombay, 1882).

Gupta, Parul, *The Banjaras of Andhra Pradesh—Effect of Urbanization on Women's Costume and their Embroidery*, MSc. Thesis, University of Delhi, Delhi, 1991.

Habib, Ifrane, 'Merchant Communities in Precolonial India' in J. D. Tracy (ed.), *The Rise of Merchant Empires* (Cambridge, 1993).

Halbar, B. G., *Lamani Economy and Society in Change* (Delhi, 1986).

— 'Socio-cultural Identity of the Lamani in the North-West Karnataka' in P. K. Misra and K. C. Malhotra (eds), *Nomads in India* (Calcutta, 1982).

Hancock, Ian, 'The Emergence of Romani as a Koïné Outside of India' in *Scholarship and the Gypsy Struggle: Commitment in Romani Studies* (Hertfordshire, 2000).

Hansen, Waldemar, *The Peacock Throne: The Drama of Mogul India* (New Delhi, 1981).

Hassan, Syed Siraj Ul, *The Castes and Tribes of H. E. H. The Nizam's Dominions* (Bombay, 1920).

Holmes, Richard, *Wellington: The Iron Duke* (London, 2002).

Ibbetson, Denzil, *Punjab Castes* (Lahore, 1916).

Iwatate, Hiroko, 'Handicraft of the Nomadic Banjara, Karnataka' in *Textiles: The Soul of India* (Tokyo, 2007).

Iyer, L. K., and Anantha Krishna, *The Mysore Tribes and Castes* (Mysore, 1928).

Keay, John, *India, A History: From the Earliest Civilizations to the Boom of the Twenty-First Century* (London, 2010).

Kennedy, Michael, *Notes on Criminal Classes in the Bombay Presidency* (Bombay, 1908).

Kenrick, Donald, *Gypsies: from the Ganges to the Thames* (Hertfordshire, 2004).

Kitts, Eustace, *Report on the Census of Berar, 1881* (Bombay, 1882).

Krishnamurthy, M., *Crimes and Customs among the Lambanis in Chitradurga District* (Dharwad, 2000).

Leigh, L., 'Vagrancy and the Criminal Law' in T. Cook (ed.), *Vagrancy: Some New Perspectives* (London, 1979).

Levi, Scott Cameron, *The Banjara: Medieval Indian Peddlers and Military Commissariat*, MA Thesis, University of Wisconsin-Madison, Madison, 1994.

Lyall, Alfred, *Asiatic Studies: Religious and Social* (London, 1884).

Macaulay, Thomas, 'Minute on Education' in Henry Sharp (ed.), *Selections from Educational Records: 1781–1839* (Calcutta, 1965).

MacKenzie, Hector, *Report of the Revised Settlement of the Goojerat District, in the Rawul Pindee Division* (Lahore, 1861).

Malcolm, John, *A Memoir of Central India* (London, 1823).

Marriott, John, and Bhaskar Mukhopadhyay (eds), *Britain in India, 1765–1905* (London, 2006).

Mandelslo, Johan Albrecht de, 'Voyages and Travels' in J. Harris (ed.), *Navigantium atque Itinerantium Bibliotheca* (London, 1666).

Mill, John, *The History of British India* (London, 1817).

Mohan, N. Shantha, *Status of Banjara Women in India (A Study of Karnataka)* (New Delhi, 1988)

Moor, Edward, *A Narrative of the Operations of Captain Little's Detachment* (London, 1794).

Morrell, Anne, *Indian Embroideries*, Part 2 (Ahmedabad, 2013).

Mullaly, Frederick S., *Notes on the Criminal Classes of the Madras Presidency* (Madras, 1892).

Mundy, Peter in Richard Carnac Temple (ed.), *The Travels of Peter Mundy in Europe and Asia 1608–1667* (London, 1914).

Narayan, Lakshmi, and Maianna von Hippel, 'Life Passages in Embroidery: The Lambani Women Artisans' in Laila Tyabji (ed.), *Threads & Voices: Behind the Indian Textile Tradition* (Mumbai, 2007).

Naik, D. B., *The Art and Literature of Banjara Lambanis* (New Delhi, 2000).

Naik, Rupla Y., *Colourful Banjara (Lambani) Tribe Through the Ages* (Bangalore, 1998).

Orme, Robert, *A History of the Military Transactions of the British Nation in Indostan* (Madras 1861).

Parmar, Shyam, *Folklore of Madhya Pradesh* (New Delhi, 1972).

Parr, Martin, and Gerry Badger, *The Photobook: A History*, (London, 2004).

Penny, F. E., *Southern India* (London, 1914).

Pratap, D. R., *Festivals of Banjaras* (Hyderabad, 1972).

Rai, Niraj, Gyaneshwer Chaubey, Tamang Rakesh et al., 'The Phyylogeography of Y-Chromosome Haplogroup H1a1a-M82 Reveals the Likely Indian Origin of the European Romani Populations' in PLoS ONE 7(11) (Cambridge, 2012).

Ramaswami, K. V. (ed.), 'Handicraft Survey Report on Banjara Embroidery' in *Census of India 1981*, part XD, series 12, Maharashtra (Nashik, 1988).

Randhawa, T. S., *The Last Wanderers: Nomads and Gypsies of India* (Ahmedabad, 1996).

Rao, Nivedita Krishna, 'Banjara Embroidery of Andhra – Origins, Development and Growth' in Jasleen Dhamija (ed.), *Asian Embroidery* (New Delhi, 2004).

Rathor, B. Shyamala Devi, 'A Comparative Study of Some Aspects of the Socio-economic Structure of Gypsy/Ghor Communities in Europe and in Andhra Pradesh, India' in *European Journal of Intercultural Studies* (London, 1996).

Regani, Sarojini, *Nizam-British Relations, 1724–1857* (New Delhi, 1988).

Rivers, Victoria Z., 'Indian Mirror Embroidery from Gujarat' in *Ornament* 16 (3) (Escondido, 1993).

— *The Shining Cloth: Dress and Adornment that Glitters* (London, 1999).

Roe, Thomas in William Foster (ed.), *The Embassy of Sir Thomas Roe to India, 1615–19* (London, 1926).

Rose, Clare, 'Banjara Embroidery Techniques' in *Embroidery*, 43 (3) (Surrey, 1992).

Rousselet, Louis, *India and its Native Princes* (London, 1875).

Russell, Robert Vane, *The Tribes and Castes of the Central Provinces of India* (London, 1916).

Seccombe, T., 'Edward Moore' in *Dictionary of National Biography*, 1885–1900.

Severn, J. Kenneth, *Architects of Empire: The Duke of Wellington and his Brothers* (Norman, 2007).

Skelton, Robin, 'A Decorative Motif in Mughal Art' in Pratapaditya Pal (ed.), *Aspects of Indian Art* (Los Angeles, 1972).

Strachey, J., and R. Strachey, *The Finances and Public Works of India* (London, 1882).

Tavernier, Jean-Baptiste in Valentine Ball and William Crooke (eds), *Travels in India* (London, 1925).

Thurston, Edgar, *Castes and Tribes of Southern India* (Madras, 1909).

Tod, James, *Annals and Antiquities of Rajasthan* (2nd edn, Madras, 1873).

Tomašević, Nebojša Bato, and Djurić Rajko, *Gypsies of the World* (London, 1989).

Untracht, Oppi, *Traditional Jewelry of India* (New York, 1997).

Varady, Robert Gabriel, 'North Indian Banjaras: Their Evolution as Transporters' in *South Asia: Journal of South Asian Studies* (London, 1979).

Washbrook, D. A., 'Progress and Problems' in P. O'Brian (ed.), *Industrialization: Critical Perspectives on the World Economy* (Oxford, 1998).

Watson, J. Forbes, and John William Kaye (eds), *The People of India* (London, 1868–75).

Wellesley, Arthur in John Gurwood (ed.), *The Dispatches of Field Marshal The Duke of Wellington during his Various Campaigns...1799 to 1818* (London, 1837).

Wilks, Mark, *Historical Sketches of the South of India* (London, 1817).

Wolpert, Stanley, *A New History of India* (7th edn, Oxford, 2004).

Index

tigers, immune from attack 41,
    101
Tipu Sultan 36, 42, 44, 46
Tod, James 57, 59, 63, 64
tourist market 93, 94, 150
trespass 53, 73
tribals 21

Udaipur 23

Vagh, Doondia 46
Varady, Robert Gabriel 83

Wellesley, Arthur (Duke of
    Wellington) 46, 47, 49, 52
Wellesley, Richard Colley
    (Marquis) 52
Wilks, Mark 12, 56

OVERLEAF
Detail of a ceremonial cloth
showing cross stitch. The full
textile may be seen on page 17.